WHAT MESSAGES ARE YOU GIVING YOUR KIDS?

WHAT MESSAGES ARE YOU GIVING YOUR KIDS?

RON WOODS

Deseret Book Company
Salt Lake City, Utah

The people and incidents portrayed in this book are fictitious. Any resemblance to actual individuals or situations is coincidental.

Library of Congress Cataloging-in-Publication Data

Woods, Ron.
   What messages are you giving your kids?

   Includes index.
   1. Parenting. 2. Child rearing. 3. Child psychology.
I. Title.
HQ755.8.W67   1987   649'.1   87-13089
ISBN 0-87579-097-6

First Printing September 1987

To Angela, David, Taylor, Matthew,
Geneal, Alysa, and Aaron—
my seven intructors in the importance
of the "little things."

Contents

Preface

If our children had sufficient vocabulary and objectivity, how would they describe us as parents? Their descriptions would probably not always fit how we see ourselves or how we want to be seen. Perhaps we would be alarmed to be rated as impatient, grouchy, demanding, or selfish. Or we might be shocked that we are seen as indifferent, judgmental, unapproachable, or preachy. We would surely merit our share of positive labels too. But on many occasions, we may radiate something other than what we suppose.

This is no great surprise to most parents. We're bound to be misperceived in a few things no matter what we do. Also, all of us display contradictions between what we say and what we do, as well as the more subtle difference between what we are and what we think we are. One of life's constant struggles is the effort to increase harmony and congruence between where we find ourselves and where we want to be.

But some parents say, "I am what I am. This is how I was raised, and this is how my children will be raised." They don't seem interested in taking steps to learn how they are viewed by others nor in changing and growing. When we take such a view, I believe we deceive ourselves. We can't progress and improve because we don't recognize our faults.

And beyond this self-stagnation, we hurt others—our own children. Because we don't know ourselves or know how others perceive us, we may not be teaching our children what we think we are teaching. These are the dangers of the so-called "unexamined life."

How much more effective we could be as parents if we watched a little more carefully the messages we send. So many interactions between parents and children—even the smallest ones—have a powerful emotional effect, either positive or negative, though we may not always recognize this at the time. If we're not attentive, the very values we want our children to adopt and cherish may come to be tinged with hidden negative overtones that can eventually result in the value itself being rejected.

When life's *big* problems occur, we often remember to be our best parental selves—patient, supportive, helpful, in control. But life is obviously filled with many more little things than big ones, and it's the ordinary daily occurrences that parents must be alert to. These small, common, even boring events of life—insignificant trivialities, we suppose them to be at the time—reveal who and what we really are. But they also teach our children what kind of people they are to become and how they are to conduct their own lives. Life really consists of the small stuff. Robert Brault said, "Pay attention to the little things, for one day you may look back and realize they were the big things."

This book will illustrate a few dozen of life's "little things" in which parents, in spite of showing concern for their children, find themselves teaching something they didn't mean to teach or missing an opportunity to impart a valuable lesson. (Occasionally, parents in these examples catch themselves doing something right, too!) Each topic will be introduced by a vignette or story in which parents may be chagrined (or pleased) to see themselves.

Following each chapter are discussion questions parents may wish to talk over with each other or their children. (Even those who are currently single parents will find these questions useful guides for further thinking about the topic and for planning improvements.)

These discussions of parenting's little things are also rather "little"—brief rather than exhaustive, suggestive of solutions rather than prescriptive—because no book can provide all the answers. Since always being a good parent is clearly a difficult task, and since each family is unique in many ways, no book or library full of books will provide all the solutions to a particular situation. However, perhaps we can help identify the problems, and that's half the battle.

I'm convinced that parents who will read a book about parenting are willing to spend time and effort at self-improvement. Once they see their own faults as part of the problem and determine to improve, they will likely find ways to become part of the solution.

Parenting is difficult, and the answers are not always clear. But one thing seems obvious about raising children: our attention to the little things will cause most of the big things to take care of themselves.

1

Perfectionism

One of the most harmful of the unintentional messages parents send their children is that perfection is the only acceptable level of performance, behavior, and obedience. We may not always mean to send that message, but our children often perceive it nonetheless. Yet psychologists tell us that a perfectionistic attitude is unhealthy and breeds dissatisfaction and unhappiness. Because we live in an imperfect world full of imperfect people, our demands for faultless performances in ourselves and others are impossible to fulfill and therefore conducive to massive intolerance of our own shortcomings.

Of course, the best *is* worth striving for. Excellence is a fine goal, but *perfection* is so far beyond *excellence* that in most human endeavors, it's simply unattainable. And when we pursue an impossible standard, we set ourselves up to fail. Instead of being happy with our accomplishments—excellent though they may be—we become upset because we didn't do more and do it better. We feel like failures because good isn't good enough, and our goal—perfection—is never reached. This produces tension and unhappiness.

To the extent that parents teach their children not to be discontented with a lack of perfection but to set realistic goals and accept their own best efforts as worthy, they will be preparing them to maintain a realistic and happy attitude toward life.

As in so much of life, it's in the little things that we often unknowingly teach perfectionism, as shown in the following five situations.

Perfectionism Is Unrealistic and Unhealthy

It's one minute to midnight, Friday night. Only one light is visible on Elm Avenue—the porch light at the Cook home. The house is quiet except for the slight but insistent wheeze of the swivel rocker in the living room where pajama-clad Bill Cook rocks vigorously.

"Calm down, Bill," says his wife, Joan, who sits across the darkened room on the sofa. "That chair sounds like it's about ready for blast-off."

Bill stops in mid-rock, suddenly aware of how his emotions are being channeled into the straining rocker. "I guess it is," he says, as the clock on the mantle strikes twelve.

"She's late," both parents say in unison. "Well, she's going to get it this time," Bill adds. "I'll ground her for a month."

Andrea Cook, sixteen, the subject of this discussion, is at this moment out on only the fourth date of her life. Her curfew for weekends is midnight, and her parents have discussed with her several times the need to be in on time. By most people's standards, Andrea has done pretty well. But her arrival times of 12:17, 11:44, and 12:04—which Bill kept meticulous track of—on her first three dates, respectively, were not acceptable to the Cooks. (Of course, if the occasion when she was early—the second date—was not a problem, neither was it praised, and now it has been forgotten by her parents.)

So this time they're going to come down hard.
Bill has decided: the minute the couple pulls into
the driveway, he will march out the door and bring
Andrea into the house.

During the next few minutes, the Cooks strain
at the sound of every distant automobile as the
rhythm of the rocker gradually increases.

Since we're not discussing dating per se, we needn't be
sidetracked by the question of the proper time for a sixteen-
year-old to come home; these matters vary from family to
family. Obviously parents may have to enforce deadlines more
stringently than teenagers might wish. Arrival times are a
common area of discussion between parents and teens, and
the Cooks shouldn't be condemned for their concern.

But these parents do have a problem—and not only in
the vigor of their planned approach (dragging their daughter
out of her date's car on the moment of arrival, thereby inflict-
ing a great deal of unnecessary embarrassment and likely
harming a relationship that may be valuable to Andrea). Their
main problem is the *intensity* with which they view the whole
matter of arrival times.

What Bill and Joan are demanding of their daughter is
nothing short of perfection. And while perfection *is* possible
in a few things, their daughter does not have complete control over her arrival time. If her parents would stop to think
about it, they would see that the two of them also occasionally find themselves in situations where punctuality is par-
tially out of their control.

For example, the Cooks have always told their children
that dinner is at six o'clock and that all the family is to be
there for it. However, Bill himself is sometimes a few minutes late getting home from work. His carpool drivers are
not consistently on time; clearly that situation is out of his
control. And although Joan is home during the day, she is
sometimes late with dinner through circumstances beyond

her control—phone calls, errands in town, special needs of the children, and her own projects, to name a few.

Yet neither parent seems to recognize that their daughter is similarly not in complete control of the situation when she is out with a young man. Her date may be fully aware that Andrea is to be home at midnight. However, movie ending times, slow service at the restaurant, traffic and driving conditions, and other things may affect return times. On her first night out a few weeks ago, for example, as Andrea and her date left the movie, they bumped into friends who insisted they drive together across town to a particular eating establishment. The time was then only ten-thirty, and there seemed no reason not to accept the invitation. Unfortunately, the driving time to the restaurant was greater than expected. Andrea found it hard to be the one to say, "I have to go now," although that is what she eventually had to do. That she was only seventeen minutes late was the result of her rather rudely scurrying her date along as they left the group.

Certainly unexpected delays can become convenient excuses. And this is not acceptable. Learning to *expect* delays so that they can compensate for them is an important lesson for young people. But the point is that the matter is not entirely in Andrea's control.

The Cooks suppose that their insistence on precise arrival times will teach Andrea to obey, to get sufficient sleep, and to keep herself from unwholesome dating situations at too late an hour, among other important positive lessons. And there is obvious value in each of these. However, the approach Bill and Joan have chosen may also teach their daughter a few things they don't want to teach: extremism and perfectionism, as well as parental rejection and a lack of trust.

When presented with such demands, Andrea has a choice. If she rejects her parents' extremism, she will widen the parent-teen gulf and bring down further repercussions on her head. If she accepts their extremism, she may create an unrealistic set of demands on herself and those around her that can lead to the unhealthy view that she is a constantly failing person.

Self-rejection and its concomitant lowering of self-image are the main dangers of perfectionistic attitudes.

Perfectionism Kills Creativity and Individuality

Mark had gone to a movie with his dad for "boy's night out" at the Darnell family. When they arrived home after ten o'clock, they found mom reading in bed.

"How was it?" she asked.

"Pretty good," dad said.

"It was great," Mark said. "I'll tell you about it."

"OK," mom said, "if you'll keep it short, let me finish this paragraph first, *and* get to bed right afterward. It's late enough for a nine-year-old to be up, even on a Saturday night."

Having gone to brush his teeth while Mark started on the plot, dad was in his pajamas and in bed before Mark got through the first scene.

"You'll have to hurry along, son," dad said. "I'm tired."

Mark went on.

"Mark, you're giving too many details," dad interrupted a moment later. "Just tell the main things or the telling will take longer than the seeing."

"OK," Mark sighed. He knew he was taking too long, but he didn't know what to leave out. "And so, when the pilot saw there was a leak in the fuel tank, he asked the copilot—"

"Oh, Mark, skip that part." Dad sounded irritated. "It doesn't matter what he said to the copilot."

"But dad, I was going to show how the copilot acted strange about it, like he didn't want to say all he knew."

"Yes, but now you've given away the biggest clue to what's wrong with the plane," dad groaned. "Anyway, keep it moving."

By now Mom had slid down from her reading position and was looking *very* comfortable, her eyelids beginning to sag. "What happened at the end, Mark?" she asked with a yawn.

"I can't tell the end yet," Mark protested. "There's a lot more before that." He went on, "So then this man in the back of the plane, one of the passengers, came up to the cockpit and he said—"

"He was a Bulgarian," dad interjected. "Don't forget, and he had a glass eye. That's important later on."

"I was going to tell that later, dad. Anyway, this Bulgarian came up and said he had to talk to the captain. But the copilot wouldn't let him. He said the captain was busy."

Dad interrupted again, "Don't forget that the man said he had information that would save the plane."

"That's just what I was going to say, dad! First, I wanted . . . " Mark was clearly frustrated. He paused a moment, then turned to his dad. "Then what, dad?"

By the time dad had summarized the rest of the plot, mom's breathing was deep and even, and she managed only a weak, "Um, sounds interesting. Get to sleep now, Mark. Good night."

The next morning at breakfast, when Mark's big sister, Laurel, asked about the movie because she had been invited to see it that night with a date, Mark said, "Oh, it's OK, I guess."

"Well, what's it about?" Laurel asked.

"Oh, it's about a plane with problems."

"A plane with problems? Is that all?"

Mark said, "Oh, there's more, but dad can tell the rest."

Most parents know the danger of inviting a youth to tell the plot of a movie at ten o'clock at night. The D-Day invasion was probably planned in less time than it takes a child to tell about a movie. Preteens are generally unable to distinguish between a major scene and a minor one. They're likely to miss key points and wrongly emphasize lesser issues, and they're certain to convolute a complex plot beyond comprehension. As to summarizing, children don't have the slightest idea how to do it.

But how much better it would have been for the Darnells to ask Mark to wait until morning to tell his story than for Dad to correct, rush, interrupt, and finally take over. The effect on Mark seems obvious by breakfast, when he is no longer interested in talking about the movie.

Of course, movie-recounting is only one example of how youth sometimes try to follow the path of their own perspective and creativity, only to find parents insisting on straightening them out.

For all our culture's espousal of creativity, there seems to be relatively little tolerance for it in some of our homes and schools. Most of us have heard the story of the first grader who was *too* creative. She was proud of her picture of a tree with purple leaves and blue trunk. "Very interesting," said her teacher. "Of course, trees aren't really purple and blue, are they?" The child soon learned that praise came only when she drew "standard" green-and-brown trees like everyone else in the class.

Sometimes we give the impression that we want to curtail our children's creativity and make them into "standard," "right-thinking" clones. We criticize what they say and how they say it; we argue against their ideas and push them to see things our way. Then, just as Mark lost interest in telling about the movie, our children lose interest in sharing their thoughts and feelings with us, and the generation gap has been widened.

Of course, there are extremes either way. And a certain amount of conformity seems required to prepare young people to be able to live with other people in the world. So it's not easy to say how far parents should go in letting children choose their own path. But we must recognize that our fears about our children not "fitting in," along with our sometimes lazy desire to keep them easy to manage, can cause us to demand too much conformity—another form of perfectionism —at the price of spontaneity and the ability to enjoy the differences in people.

Perfectionism Chases Away the Volunteers

When eight-year-old Jill came home after school, mom was at the kitchen counter. Giving her mom a kiss, Jill said, "I want to help."

"OK, honey. Put your book bag away and wash your hands first."

When Jill came back to the kitchen, she asked, "What are you making?"

"First I have to make a green salad to send over to the Wilsons tonight. Mrs. Wilson is sick, so Mary Higley and I are taking in dinner to the family. Then I hope there will be time to make cookies for us as well as for them."

"Let me make the cookies first," Jill said, bringing a small stool to the counter to stand on.

"No, we have to have the salad ready when Mary comes to pick it up. Why don't you get out the things for the salad while I work on our own dinner?"

"OK," Jill said, as she hopped down and went to the refrigerator for the lettuce and other vegetables.

"Don't slam the fridge door," mom cautioned.

Jill gathered the ingredients and reached for the food shredder. "No, just break the lettuce by hand this time, Jill. That will be faster."

As Jill worked, mom continued to instruct. "That's too big; break it smaller." "That's not enough; do more." "It's too wet; shake it dry."

Jill's protest that she knew how to do the job didn't help much. Other directions came as Jill proceeded with the other vegetables. "Don't peel that carrot so deep; you're wasting half of it." "Cut those tomatoes smaller, and don't get juice on your clothes." "Mix it better."

When the salad was made, mom said, "OK, good. Now get the recipe cards and find the raisin cookies we like."

"I don't like those very well, mom. I like—"

"But they're easy to make and most people like them, so let's do those."

"I'm tired of cooking, mom," Jill said. "I don't want to do any more." She put away her stool and went outside to play.

Mom shook her head and said to herself, "That girl just doesn't have any sticking power. She always quits before the job is through."

What mom doesn't realize is that her very bossiness—her perfectionistic approach, we might call it—is what's causing Jill to enjoy less and less the time she spends helping around the house. There is certainly a need for instruction in any task, and parents can teach a great deal about work by working with their children. However, while each comment made by mom may seem innocuous in itself, their sum total is an overwhelming load of meddlesome, censorious imperatives that are most unpleasant to be around. They are certainly more than what is needed for quality instruction, and they seem to say, "My way is the only right way."

If mom continues this approach in other tasks Jill does with her, the result is inevitable. Jill's offers to help will occur less frequently until, finally, mom will find that getting Jill to help is a bigger chore than doing the job herself. The joyous days of youthful volunteerism will be gone forever.

Punctuality and Pre-planning

It's 8:31 Sunday morning and church starts at 9:00. The chapel is only a few blocks away, but the Higgins family needs to be in the car in exactly fourteen minutes if they're to be sure of being on time. Unfortunately, the morning is turning into a rush that has become typical for Sunday.

"Mommy, I can't find my shoes," five-year-old Ted calls from his room.

"Mom, Marie isn't ready to help me yet. Can you do my hair or do I have to wait for her?" asks eight-year-old Alice.

Dad comes into the bathroom where mom is changing the baby's diaper. "Honey, I can't find any pants for the baby. Has the laundry been brought up?"

Not waiting for an answer, he adds, "I have to go anyway. Brother Hart called and wants to meet with me for a minute before priesthood meeting. I won't have time to come back for you, so I'll take the little car. May I borrow your keys? I think Marie has mine. 'Bye." To his wife's exasperated sigh, he says, "Good luck," and out the door he goes.

Bud, thirteen, is late getting up and wants to know why no one saved him any orange juice. His unpolished shoes are in the hall where mom dropped them last night with the suggestion that he shine them. Parley, ten, is planning to dress as soon as he finishes the comics in the Sunday paper; he will need help tying his tie. And Marie, sixteen, who's supposed to use the curling iron on Alice's hair on Sunday mornings, will barely have time to get herself ready, since she's only now getting out of bed.

Mother is upset! She needs to be at church at least five minutes early to talk with the Primary chorister about today's music. She needs to finish dressing herself, yet since no one else in the family is ready, she can expect no help with the smaller children.

Let's leave the story for a moment so our gaze can be averted from mom's reaction to this crisis. It isn't lovely to see. And by the time the family arrives at the church building, three minutes late, Parley's tie is still not tied, Bud is grouchy because he got no juice, Marie is resentful because she had to take time from her own last-minute grooming to curl Alice's hair and to find dad's keys for mom to use, and Ted is dejectedly tying his sneakers, since he never found his Sunday shoes. No one is happy about going to church, except perhaps the baby, who is oblivious to the problems about him, and dad, who escaped early.

Imagine this scene being repeated nearly every Sunday morning, week after week, during a child's formative years. Since Sunday mornings at the Higgins house produce tension, stress, hard feelings, occasional tears, anger, and frustration, and since none of these feelings are much fun, over time these Sunday morning blues are likely to affect the way a child feels about attending church.

Just as some adults reject church because they were forced, in a negative way, to attend as children, some may reject it for even more subtle reasons, such as bad feelings related to Sunday morning preparation, and their additional perception that mom and dad always seemed frustrated in getting to meetings. They might come to the conclusion, reasonable from their experience, that church isn't a very fine thing after all and maybe just not worth the trouble. The Higgins may think they are teaching their children a positive lesson—that it's important to be on time. They may, however, be teaching an entirely different—and negative—lesson about church itself.

Though this episode has dealt with the specific situation of preparing for church, the same idea may apply to getting ready for other places on time. Consider mealtimes, school, work, shopping, and vacations. How we prepare for them may greatly affect how our children view them. Our efforts at efficiency and promptness may exact a great cost in removing fun and spontaneity from the event, ultimately causing family members to lose interest in the activity itself.

Punctuality is often important, but it's doubtful that it ever need be an end in itself. And if it is to be achieved, it requires advance planning. The costs of seeking perfection in punctuality *without* planning are just not worth the negative feelings engendered.

Some Things Really Don't Matter Much

"What on earth is that?" dad bellowed when Kent came home from the barbershop.

Dad took Kent by the shoulders and turned him around. He stared at the back of Kent's neck, where a narrow wisp of long hair pointed straight down toward the floor. "I think the barber played a trick on you, Kent."

"It's just a tail, dad," sighed Kent. "Don't freak out. Haven't you ever seen one?"

"Where would I see a thing like that, except on an armadillo?"

"On TV, I guess."

"Not only have I never seen one, I've never heard of one, and, speaking of freaks, I will certainly not have my thirteen-year-old son walking around looking like one—even if they do on TV," dad said as he headed for the drawer where the scissors were kept. "I'm taking that thing off right now."

"Oh, no you're not, dad," Kent retorted. "I paid twelve dollars for this styling."

"Styling!" dad sputtered. "First it's tails, now it's styling. I will not have any man from this house paying good money for hair styling. *Women* get hair styling; *men* get haircuts. Now, come here and let me finish the job."

Let's stop the action right there. One of the frustrating and humbling things about parenting is that many of the things we feel are important—even vital—in raising our children, often appear later to have mattered very little.

If dad were to wise up a minute, he might avoid an unnecessary confrontation over what will later seem a very minor issue. Dad feels challenged by Kent's bizarre hairstyle, and it is true that dad's former, seemingly stable world is being challenged in many ways these days. But it isn't really Kent who's challenging it—it's society at large. Kent is only experimenting with a style he's seen. It's likely that, deep down, dad fears his son is becoming a sissy or in some way not following the "standard" path to manhood.

What dad may have forgotten or never have recognized is that in our culture today, there is no standard path to maturity, at least not a perfectly marked one. If that constitutes a problem, it's one of the prices we pay for the great personal freedom and individuality most of us expect and demand and which our society affords us. In this country, we all don't have to take the same route.

Certainly we parents are free to state our views—even about new hairstyles. Yet, after so stating, how much do we insist that our opinion become the only acceptable one in the house? The more perfectionistic we are, the more demanding we will be that our children follow our views, and the more we will stifle their growth. Sometimes parents *do* need to stifle certain processes, but they need to be sure that each demand is worth that cost.

Hair and clothing styles are surely among those things that are furthest from moral absolutes. Of course, most people would concede that there are implicit dangers in certain extremes of style—as there are in all extremes—the main danger being the kinds of friends who might be attracted by a particular style. Styles often do send a "message." Still, care ought to be used not to assign absolutes in such a volatile, shifting sphere as fashion. Styles come and go so quickly. Some of them have even reversed their messages in recent years. For example, the rebellion shown by long hair on males in the '70's has, in the '80's, been somewhat restated in extremely short hair. The beards of the '60's supposedly meant defiance; now, in many parts of the country, they have almost become a requisite mark of style for the most conservative professional men.

When the father in the example gives the matter some thought, he will recognize that so many things change from generation to generation that Kent's experiments with hairstyles are not necessarily more dangerous in themselves than dad's own long-past youthful obeisance to white socks, ducktails, and rat-tail combs jutting rakishly from hip pockets. He can then spend his discussion time with his son on the important issues Kent may need answers to, and ignore many of the lightweight matters—like tails on haircuts—that will surely pass as quickly as a summer evening's thunderstorm.

Questions for Discussion

Realizing that children will sometimes take things further than parents intend them, do we see trends in our children to indicate that they have taken our desires for high achievements to unrealistic levels?

How can we teach our children that we love them even if they aren't perfect? How can we let them know that we make mistakes too and that, as their parents, we also need *their* love and understanding?

How do we rate ourselves at allowing others to be themselves and not demanding conformity in things that don't matter? How much do we see individualism as a positive trait to be cherished and nurtured? In what areas is conformity important to us? In what areas could we allow greater freedom and individuality?

How closely do we agree on what constitutes "best efforts" and "excellence" as opposed to "perfection"? Are our children learning to avoid working with us because of demands for perfection in chores?

In our home, is there a negative atmosphere in preparing for church meetings or other events? Is there a tolerable level of tardiness—at least occasionally—that really need not ruin our day? Or is being on time an absolute? Is there a difference in being late to a function where others are inconvenienced by waiting on us, and in being late to a larger gathering where the group can begin without us? Is part of the problem that the two of us don't agree on these concepts of the "morality" of punctuality? If we decide to make changes in our routine, what problems will be solved and what new ones might arise? How will these be handled?

Without abrogating our positions as parents by saying "anything goes," how can we increase our long-range perspective on what really matters?

2

Basic Values

Most parents want to teach their children to be honest and ethical, kind and helpful to others, hard working, optimistic, and willing to put others before material things. They want them to demonstrate the many virtues that combine to produce what society labels as "good" people. But we deceive ourselves if we suppose that such values are taught only when we sit down to give a home-evening lesson or make a point during a dinner-table discussion. Since most of the values we hold are quite visible in our interactions with others, we do most of our teaching through our everyday actions. We're watched by our children much more than we might want to be. They observe and learn even when we don't realize we're teaching. This constant scrutiny may sometimes be disturbing. However, we can't do much about it—except to use it as a positive teaching tool to make sure we exemplify the ethical standards we want our children to notice and adopt.

Not that giving those prepared lessons about integrity, charity, and hard work will hurt; they may help a great deal to define and clarify. But it's when we're caught *unprepared* that we demonstrate our true values. We mustn't fool ourselves that formal lessons—where we *say* what we believe—will be as lasting as our daily actions—where we *show* what we believe.

A list of virtues parents might like their children to adopt could become very long indeed. The five chosen for inclusion here are merely illustrative of the kinds of values that are so easy to talk about yet often difficult to consistently teach by example.

Ethics: So Easy to Talk About

"Listen to this, dad," Tom called from the living room. "The headline says 'Convict Develops Cop Detector.' "

Phil left the kitchen, where he was helping his wife clean up dinner dishes, and joined his son, who was sprawled on the floor over the afternoon paper.

" 'London. Police today arrested a convicted felon with a police detection device the man admits to inventing,' " Tom read. " 'Hugh O'Casey, alias Scott O'Day, three-time convicted burglar, was arrested in the act of breaking and entering a London townhouse in the early dawn this morning when a bobby walking the beat happened upon him. In O'Casey's possession was a mysterious battery-powered black box. When questioned at police headquarters, the burglar seemed proud to demonstrate the ingenious device which sets off a flashing red light when a police cruiser is within a range of three to four blocks, giving the burglar time to hide or get away.' Isn't that amazing?" Tom asked excitedly.

"I wonder how that thing works," Phil mused.

"That's right here," Tom went on. "It says, 'It seems O'Casey had created a type of radar device sensitive to the shortwave radios used in the police cars—even when they're not broadcasting. He told police he had planned to abandon the breaking and entering trade and go into underground production of these devices as soon as the prototype was perfected—for sale to his colleagues in the trade.' "

"Unbelievable," sighed Phil. "What the crooks won't think of next."

"And here's the funny part, dad," said Tom, resuming his reading: " 'It appears O'Casey might have gotten away with this morning's heist if his black box had just been able to detect a footsore flatfoot walking the beat. O'Casey's main concern upon arrest was that he be allowed to patent his plan so no one could steal the idea while he served time for the burglary charge.' "

Phil saw his moment to make a point with his impressionable nine-year-old. "Yes, Tom, that makes an interesting story, but let's not forget that the whole thing is disturbing, too. I mean, here's a man using his God-given brains to invent machines to help him circumvent the law. Don't you find that sad?"

"Well, yes," Tom said, "But it's still interesting." He had already moved on to the sports page as Phil returned to the kitchen.

"Did you hear that?" he said to his wife, Arlene. "Isn't it amazing what people will do to get around the law?"

"Yes, I heard," she said. After a pause and a quick glance at her husband, she asked rhetorically, "It almost sounds like the radar detector in your car, doesn't it?"

"Why, no," Phil said. "They work on entirely different principles."

"I don't mean how they work. I'm just talking about their purpose. You know, to warn violators of the presence of officers." Arlene had her back to him and her hands in the sink, and Phil couldn't see her face.

"Are you comparing that . . . that *criminal* device with a simple . . . uh . . . speed warning instrument?" he sputtered.

"Just asking if they were similar."

"Why, everybody has one of those things these days . . . " Phil began. He was becoming vaguely aware that this discussion was inexorably pushing him into a recognition he didn't want to make. Therefore, he was relieved to hear the ringing of the phone on the wall beside him. He grabbed the receiver on the first ring.

"Yes . . . yes, this is the place for sale," he said. "It's about the house," Phil whispered to Arlene.

"Oh, good," she said. Since Phil and Arlene had had their house up for sale for months with very few inquiries, it was exciting to have a caller. While Phil talked, Arlene finished her work and went to the living room, hoping to get a section of the newspaper from Tom.

When he hung up a few minutes later, Phil came into the room and said, "Those people are very interested in looking through the house. They saw the realtor's sign in the yard today but didn't have time to stop. They tried to call the realtor tonight and got no answer, but they managed to find our number—saw our family name on the plaque over the door, I think, and looked us up in the phone book. Very clever. Just the kind of people I'd like to deal with."

Phil sat down. "So I told them *not* to call the realtor. His contract with us expires in a few days anyway, and you know he hasn't done a thing to get this house moving in all these months. I told them to come and see the house tomorrow, but, if they're interested in making an offer, to wait until next week and I would lower the price the amount

of the realtor's fee and split the difference with
them."

"Is that legal?" Arlene asked.

"Just as legal, I'd say, as my handy radar detector, if it's done right," Phil retorted with a smug smile.

Phil certainly seems to have everything clear in his mind,
doesn't he? Or does he simply not want to think very hard
about these issues? It's easier, after all, to accept conven-
tional wisdom—to do what others do—than to have to look
into one's own conscience for answers.

What Tom thinks of all this is unclear, but one thing is
certain: much of what he comes to view as honest and ethical will be affected by what he sees and hears at home.

As a parent, Phil may someday face an interesting
dilemma. Since he finds dodging the law an acceptable way
to handle speeding, will he be as understanding if, in a few
years, his son decides using illegal drugs is OK—as long as
he doesn't get caught, of course? Since Phil thinks circum-
venting the realtor's contract to be acceptable business practice, will he also approve if Tom eventually finds his own
rationalized ways of stealing?

My own bias about radar detectors and real-estate contracts is obvious, and there may be counterarguments. Certainly ethical issues are often debatable. Sometimes much
depends on the circumstances and the context. That's why
they seem so hard to teach to children.

However, though answers aren't always clear or easy,
parents must be willing to question and confront—and teach
their children to confront—society's standardized, often lazy
ways of thinking. No parents ever let their children get very
far with the infirm excuse, "But everybody does it." Why
should parents get any further with it?

Parents must teach their children to reject slick phrasing
and "soft" language that cloud the issues. "Everybody does
it," for example, is an avoidance phrase that deflects us from
looking at the matter at hand. Note Phil's similarly sloppy

terminology: his description of his own black box as a "speed-warning instrument" compared to his labels of the convict's apparatus as a "machine to circumvent the law" and "that criminal device."

Children can learn to be careful that their approaches to problems are honest and meaningful ones. Arlene's query to Phil about his radar device was logical and reasonable, but her question about the realtor's contract was a misguided, "Is it legal?" (which brought the "If it's done right" response) rather than the more searching "Is it right?"

Children who grow up in homes where ethics are discussed will attain the skills necessary for making their own sound moral decisions rather than blithely glossing over uncomfortable issues.

In a country where millions of dollars have been spent on devices to allow law-breaking drivers to avoid speeding tickets, where contracts have to be written in pages and pages of precise legal language in an attempt to avoid all conceivable means of default (and still often end up in court), where employers often question why some of the best business schools and universities fail to teach ethics to their students, parents must be extra cautious about the quality of ethical training their children receive in the home.

Choosing People Over Things

"Well, son?" Bob called when he heard Aaron come in the door from a job interview his sister had driven him to.

"I didn't get it, dad," Aaron said as he quickly went down the front stairs. "Not this year."

"Oh, dear," said mom. She got up to follow Aaron to his room.

"Wait a minute, Louise," Bob said. "Let him alone a minute, then we'll go down and talk to him. He must be pretty broken up. He really wanted that job."

Louise sat down again. "You're right," she said. "Although he sounded awfully cheerful about it, with his 'Not this year.' "

"I wonder what went wrong," Bob mused.

Aaron, at fourteen, was ready for summer work, and the airport job looked ideal. Watering and taking care of the grounds at the resort town's small community airport over the summer would provide Aaron $100 a month, keep him close to home, and still leave him plenty of time for summer activities. As a member of the volunteer airport committee, Bob had helped screen the applicants. And of the five boys who'd applied, Aaron seemed the most qualified. He'd watered and mowed his own and neighbors' yards for years, his daily paper route had honed his dependability, his unusual size and strength made him extra capable for his age, and he would be in town all summer except for one week of scout camp.

"I feel like calling John or Ray to see what the problem was," Bob said. "When I disqualified myself from the committee as the father of one of the applicants, I had the impression that they had already agreed that Aaron was the boy." Bob started for the phone, then changed his mind. "No, I should talk to Aaron first, I guess. Louise, let's go see him now. Maybe he at least knows who got the job."

Downstairs, Bob and Louise offered their condolences to Aaron, who seemed relatively unconcerned about the whole matter, then asked who had been hired.

"Clark Jones?" Dad was incredulous. "Why, I guess Clark is a good kid and all, but, from his application, I don't think he's had the experience you've had. Did they give any reason?"

"Oh, I don't know," Aaron said, seemingly reticent to answer. He picked up his old baseball glove, neglected over the winter, and began to punch and knead it into shape.

"Didn't you speak up and tell them how badly you wanted the job? I warned you about being confident and presenting yourself well, Aaron."

"Oh, I think I did OK on that, dad," Aaron replied.

"I just don't understand," mom shook her head.

"I am going to call John," Bob said with irritation in his voice. "I want to hear him tell me how they could find Clark Jones better qualified than Aaron Roper. It doesn't make sense. Why, I'm sure Clark hasn't had any sprinkler experience or used a riding mower." Bob stood.

"No, dad, don't do that," Aaron said. "Don't call anyone. Sit down and I'll tell you why Clark got the job."

Bob sat back down on the bed.

"You have to promise you'll never tell," Aaron added.

Mom looked quizzically at her son. "Never tell? Why the secret?"

"I wasn't going to tell even you guys. And I asked the men on the committee not to tell. That would ruin everything."

Bob was puzzled. "What in the world are you talking about, son?"

"Well, see, I wanted that job really bad, you know, so I could get a new mitt and some other things, but Clark Jones, well, I knew he needed it more than I did," Aaron said. "You know his folks are having problems in their business. I heard Clark talking the other day, and he said he would have to buy all of his school clothes and pay his own school fees this fall. So, I decided and . . . well, when the committee offered me the job tonight, I asked who was the runner-up, if I didn't take it. When they said the next in line was probably Clark Jones, I felt really good about saying, 'Then I'm not taking the job. I want you to give it to Clark.' "

Bob and Louise looked at one another as their son went on. "They asked me why I would do this. So I told them why Clark needed the job. Then I said I would help him with the sprinkler system, to get him started. They sent me out of the room for a minute. When they called me back, they said OK and said they would call Clark. Then they all shook my hand and I came home. That's it."

"Wonderful, son, wonderful," Louise said.

"I don't know what to say." Bob cleared his throat. "We're very proud of you, son. Let me shake your hand, too."

How surprising it is, at first, to learn major lessons from our children. But it happens.

In our competitive world, it's easy to forget there is more to life than always being first, earning more, and climbing higher. It's easy for our children to forget their obligations to others. The home is really where these things are best taught. All of our children have a right to learn that people come first and to experience the joy that comes through giving of themselves.

Wise parents will look for teaching moments when they can reinforce their children's youthful generosity and kindness just as did Bob and Louise as they showed their son they were thrilled at his concern for others. Whether or not Aaron gets a particular job this particular summer won't likely have much effect on how he succeeds in life. But how he feels about other people and how much he is willing to go out of his way to help them will have an enormous effect on how he succeeds in the eternities.

The Lure of Materialism

Eight boys and their two leaders were enjoying
the campfire on their last night at scout camp. The
hour was late, and even the normally boisterous
scouts were subdued. Somehow the leaders had
started a conversation about the financial burden of
supporting their families.

"I can hardly keep up with things, Jim. Why, I
haven't yet paid off last Christmas." While he
talked, Chuck idly stirred the coals with a stick.

Jim said, "It seems funny talking about Christmas in the middle of July. And what you say about
paying off last Christmas is a little foreign to me,
Chuck. At our house, we've never gone into debt
for Christmas."

"You haven't?" Chuck was incredulous. "I do
every year. How do you do it? I just have to. When
I look at all the things my neighbors give their kids
for Christmas—skis and boots, motorcycles, four-
wheelers, stereos, hunting rifles—"

"Vic even got a car," interjected Chuck's boy,
Craig, as he stood and put another log on the fire.

"Yes, that's right, even a brand-new car last
year, three houses down, for their sixteen-year-old,"
Chuck resumed. "Well, when I see things like that, I
feel like I have to do all I can so my own kids don't
feel too bad. Of course, I can't match all the stuff I
see around my neighborhood, but I have to try a
little bit. And you ought to hear my kids moan as
it is. I don't see how you manage. You must have a
lot of extra cash at Christmastime. I sure don't."

Jim weighed his next answer carefully before
speaking. "Chuck, I don't want you to feel I'm putting you down or trying to sound self-righteous or
something. You've described a Christmas that might
be fine for you. But I won't do it that way. It's not

that we have extra cash at Christmas; it's that we just don't spend that much.

"When I see what some of my neighbors do at Christmas and even at other times in the year, instead of following suit, I use it as an opportunity to teach my kids to expect less, to share more, and to appreciate what they have. With a big family, I tell them our Christmas will be nice, but limited. Oh, I'm sure they feel a bit neglected at times, yet I don't sense any major disappointments. I just won't go into debt for Christmas."

"That's amazing. I don't know if I could get away with it in my family now," Chuck said. "I guess I should have started when they were younger. Come to think of it, I loved Christmas as a kid, although I never had any very elaborate presents." It was quiet for a moment as both men thought about the Christmases of their youth.

Jim decided to bring the boys into the conversation. "What do you think, boys? I know if you tried, you could all make long lists of all the things you want, but, be honest now, are expensive gifts all that important at Christmas?"

Such a discussion has a good chance of revealing that young people enjoy Christmas primarily because it's a family occasion and a chance to share. Oh, there is certain to be a selfish thought or two at times, as youth compare themselves to peers with more ostentatious rewards. But young people can be helped to see that more goodies don't necessarily make happier people.

Of course, Christmas isn't the only issue here. Chuck has bought into the commercialization of Christmas in a big way, but more than that, he's become part of what most of us experience to one degree or another in our society: the lure of the prevailing materialism of our age.

Youth is the best time to learn what may be the main flaw in the worship of material things: the gods of materialism are never satisfied. Therefore, a dedicated materialist is never happy for long, because new "toys" are marketed every day, so there is always more to covet.

Much of what parents say and do can either tell their children that money is the most important thing on earth or that it's merely a servant. Wise parents will teach that money is neither good nor bad in itself. It can open doors, provide opportunities, and accomplish good and enjoyable things. Yet it must never become an object of worship—which it tends to do when we sell ourselves into slavery to it by living beyond our means.

A movie actress described her reaction on receiving her first big check: "When I first came into money, I bought myself a mink stole which I had wanted for years. I had always thought that stole would bring me the greatest happiness in the world. Well, I enjoyed it very, very much—for about twenty minutes. After that, it was clear I didn't need it at all."

There's still time for Chuck to pull back somewhat from the excess spending he claims not to enjoy and to teach his children that the owning of more things has no direct bearing on happiness. Parents sometimes feel they have to prove their love to their children by the amount of money they spend on them. Children have always known that love doesn't equate with the amount of money their parents spend, but more on the gifts of time and self.

By the Sweat of Their Brow

It's Saturday morning at the Barlow's. Mom announced last night that today from nine until noon was to be a family workday. The plan was to complete difficult housecleaning not covered by the normal weekly and daily chore assignments.

"If we all work hard, we can get a tremendous amount done," she said. "And working together will be fun." Not all of the children were as thrilled with the prospects as mom was, though there was general agreement to help out.

Dad added, "And when we're through—if we've worked really hard—we'll go out for hamburgers for lunch."

Mom had Saturday's regular pancake breakfast ready at eight o'clock and called everyone to get up and eat. At nine o'clock, five were present, two absent.

"We'll start anyway," mom said, as she passed out assignment sheets.

"That's not fair," said Sue. "Tad and Lorraine get out of work just by getting up late?"

"I called them," mom said. "We'll just have to start and I'll roust them in a minute."

"It's not fair."

And that was only the beginning of difficulties. Over the next three hours, these were a few of the other comments heard:

Jenny: "Hey, I'm cleaning this mirror. Get away from it."

Sue: "You're not cleaning it right. Look at these spots."

Jenny: "Mom, Sue streaked the mirror I cleaned. I'm not going to clean it again."

Sue: "Aren't Tad and Lorraine here yet? They're not going to get lunch, are they, dad?"

Dad: "Quit worrying about other people. Just do a good job and learn to enjoy working."

Sue: "Well, good morning, Lorraine, my sleeping beauty. So nice of you to join us. It's only 9:45. You probably won't get lunch."

Lorraine: "Then why should I work at all? Besides, I'm not ready to work yet. I have to comb my hair. I can't help it if my alarm didn't go off."

Sue: "Oh, sure. Mom called you at eight o'clock."

Lorraine: "I guess I didn't hear her. I was tired."

Sue: "You'll still have to do the list mom made for you, even if it takes you all night."

Jenny: "Mom, Joey is splashing water all over the room. He's too little to wipe walls. Mom, now he's bawling 'cause I took away his sponge. The carpet's soaked."

Jenny: "Mom, Sue put Ajax in my hair."

Sue: "I didn't mean to, silly. It'll come out."

Jenny: "Yeah, and my hair with it."

Sue: "Dad, it's not fair. I've been working all morning. Now it's after ten, and Lorraine is just now eating breakfast. And where's Tad?"

Dad: "I just woke him up and told him to get up here. He said he didn't know anything about this project."

Sue: "Oh, sure."

Dad: "Lorraine, stop eating right now and get in here and work."

Lorraine: "What about Tad? Why should I work if he isn't?"

Dad: "Lorraine, do what I tell you. Tad will be along."

Lorraine: "Oh, sure."

Dad: "Honey, did Tad know about this last night? He says he didn't."

Mom: "I thought everyone was told. Maybe he wasn't here then, come to think of it."

Lorraine: "Mom, Jenny used up all the Ajax on one sink. How am I supposed to—"

Mom: "Oh, my. The can was nearly half full, too. Well, there's more under the sink."

Lorraine: "There's the phone. I'll get it."

Tad: "How come everybody's mad at me? I didn't even know about all this. Nobody tells me anything."

Sue: "You'll have to work twice as hard or you won't get any lunch."

Tad: "I didn't even get any breakfast."

Tad: "Dad, Lorraine's been on the phone for a half-hour. It's not fair."

Dad: "More like five minutes, son. I've never heard so much griping. Tad, you've missed an hour and a half's work, so I wouldn't be too worried about what's fair. Lorraine, get off the phone."

Lorraine: "Mom, Elizabeth's mom wants to take her to the mall, and she wants me to go."

Mom: "That will be fine, Lorraine, after we finish work."

Lorraine: "But, mom, they need to pick me up right at noon, and I'll need time to get ready."

Mom: "Then the answer is no. We're going to work this morning. It's a family event, and we were all told about the plan."

Tad: "I wasn't."

Lorraine: "I never get to do anything."

Sue: "Oh, sure."

Teaching children the value of work has to be one of the most important roles parents have. Few skills are more important than knowing how to work hard, since life offers few successes without it. However, work is often a most difficult thing to teach.

Those who have tried workathons like the Barlows will probably agree that the comments listed here barely scratch the surface of the things that can go wrong. The most carefully planned family projects can turn to disaster. There's a lot to be learned by the experience, though—mostly by mom, who learns to do all the work herself.

By noon, a few jobs are done, several more are half done, and additional new ones are necessitated by the messes made. Mom (and anyone else she can lasso) will spend the afternoon finishing up. As for lunch, how can anyone possibly decide who earned it?

As seen in the Barlow experience, feelings of unfairness and negativism can become associated with work because of poor planning, improper supervision, and a lack of coordination of effort. If we're not careful, we may think we're teaching our children to work, when we may actually be teaching them to hate work, avoid work, or do sloppy work. Without careful attention, how easily children learn that the diligent, the competent, and the willing are overused and often unthanked, while the reluctant, the slow, and the sloppy get out of the hard jobs. And that isn't fair to either group.

It's too much to expect children to learn to work and to enjoy it merely by telling them to—just as well tell a cat to enjoy swimming. Children need to be shown. They need to see a project organized and carried through to the end, and they need to see their parents taking pleasure in work and the rewards of a completed task.

Many children who were excellent workers in their youth later lost interest and became slovenly and undependable. Why? Somewhere along the way they lost their sense of achievement and reward. What was fun became drudgery. Perhaps the parental praise given them as toddlers was replaced by parental expectations and lack of reward. All of us, adults as well as children, work for rewards, and one of the strongest rewards of all is the feeling of having achieved.

Children need to feel that their work is important, not just something no one else will do. When kids get only the dirty and menial jobs, they may soon come to believe that work is some kind of punishment for being small. Why can't a child learn to bake rolls as well as learn to clean the oven? To push the lawnmower as well as empty the hopper or rake up the cut grass? To trim shrubs in the spring sunshine as well as scrub floors in the dark basement?

Parents would do well to consider four simple principles for teaching children to work: show them how, work with them, praise them, and let them see the value of their accomplishments.

Hope and Optimism

"My Sunday School teacher said today he was convinced the world would end by the year 2000. Let's see, I'd only be about twenty-six then. Is he right, dad?"

Jean's dinner-table question caught dad with a bite of roast half-chewed. In the pause while dad swallowed, Jean's older brother Mac said, "I don't know if that's right or not. My seminary teacher says we can't be sure of the date. But what bugs me about the whole thing is that some of the kids at school are so convinced it's going to happen that they say, 'Why should I plan on a career or marriage or anything? It's all going to end anyway.' I don't think that's right, is it?"

Dad was ready to respond now. "These are important questions. There are lots of different views of these matters, and your mom might have an opinion different from mine, so I'll tell you how I see things if you will recognize that it's only my opinion.

"To Jean's question, we could probably stop and analyze what is meant by the term 'the end of the world,' but if we're talking about the end of life on earth as we know it—through war or calamity or the second coming of Christ—my opinion is that we really don't know when that will be. The year 2000 is a convenient, round number, and I've heard some pretty good arguments for it. But—here's my opinion—I personally doubt that 2000 is a firm, irrevocable date."

"Brother Nichols seemed convinced of it," Jean said as she poured herself more milk.

Mom added, "Well, honey, he's allowed to feel that way. We can have our opinions, you know, as long as we don't insist that everyone else agree with us."

"That's right," dad said. "Now, Mac's question is, to me, the major one. The real issue is not so much *when* it will happen as what we should do about life in the meantime. I've heard that a lot of kids today are so sure a nuclear war is coming, for instance, that they've given up on any plans of their own. They're just waiting for the end. This way of thinking scares me a great deal."

"I think they're using it as an excuse, dad," said Mac.

Mom added, "Yes, I think it's just a reason to be lazy and not make any plans."

"I'm sure that's the case in most instances," dad continued. "But my concern is that even LDS kids sometimes talk like we're all to be blown up, so there's no hope. And that is such a ridiculous misunderstanding of the whole thing! If there's anything we know about the Second Coming—the end of the world, if you want to call it that—it's that it gives us hope in salvation and brings us joy. To twist that around to mean we *give up* hope is perverse indeed."

"But dad," Mac said, "some people are so negative. A couple of teachers at school talk like our whole generation is worthless and so the world has no chance."

Some adults, even some who think of themselves as optimists, don't realize how pessimistic many of their comments about the future or about life in general may sound to others, particularly to children. It's ironic that one of the most hopeful signs a Christian enjoys—that the Lord has promised to come again—has been so often twisted into a message of foreboding and apprehension.

Since so much of what young people hear can be alarming or depressing to them, parents need to take opportunities to develop in their children positive, optimistic, hopeful attitudes toward life. Children can learn that, although we don't know precisely what tomorrow will bring, faith and hope will carry us much further than fear and negativism. A positive outlook will brighten, enlarge, and give direction to everything our children do, while the opposite view will derail their happiness at every turn.

If we can help our children know that life is up to them and that they must not use excuses of *any* kind not to prepare for it the best they can, they will be better prepared for whatever might come.

Questions for Discussion

Are there major ethical issues we differ on as a couple? Are we clear on how we would like our children to see issues of honesty and integrity? Are there signs that we are failing in our teaching of these concepts? Are there signs of success?

How can we increase in our children behavior that puts others first? Have we praised this behavior when we've seen it occur?

Do we see danger signs in the way our children seem to view money and material things? How can we better teach them that material goods are important yet must not become all-important?

What kind of workers are we raising? Do we see a need in individual children to increase their appreciation of work as the best means of accomplishing their goals and succeeding in life?

Do we radiate optimism about the future? Are our children overly fearful or dejected when they think of their own futures? How can we help them be more hopeful?

As parents, could we benefit from spending time listing other values we want our children to learn and ways we could consciously teach these values?

3

Self-Esteem

A child's self-esteem hangs by a fragile thread. In children's earliest years, their self-concept is a reflection of how they think their parents view them. If their parents think they're great and *if the children know* they think so, they'll tend to think so too. If children don't believe their parents think so, the effect is the same as if the parents don't—the children will have trouble thinking they're worth much.

Children develop very finely honed competitive instincts, and in school they do a lot of comparing themselves to others. This constant measuring—conscious and unconscious—of themselves with others is really their way of learning who they are.

But children can't be objective about their comparisons; even more so than adults, they see others only through themselves. It's true that our view of who we are colors everything. We see the world we're programmed to see, and our self-image is the filter through which we look at the world. Sometimes, sadly, even when others think Billy is pretty good at something, he still may not believe it himself if his self-image isn't high enough to allow a positive self-acceptance. Facts alone, even positive ones, simply aren't enough to change the way he sees himself, at least not in those early years when his objectivity is so limited. And with each year that passes, his view of himself becomes more and more fixed. Changing a poor self-image past the years of early youth is like changing sails on a ship in the middle of a typhoon at sea—possible but very difficult.

Children don't realize they don't have to be good at everything. While mature adults can accept certain weaknesses and honestly say that many of them don't matter to them, children see their shortfalls only as failings. Unlike adults who, for example, might say, "I never was very good at math; big deal," when Billy's math assignments *never* come back from the teacher with a "smiley-face" on them, another scratch has been made in the lens through which the boy views himself and the world. If this view becomes too foggy and blurred through too many scratches on the lens of self-esteem, children can come to believe that they are not deserving members of society.

Parents have to keep that lens polished, to burnish out those mars and nicks, so their children can see the world clearly, and particularly so they can see themselves as worthy participants and contributors to the goals and struggles of humanity. Keeping the lens clear and bright is a daily matter of watching the little things, as shown in the following examples.

Praise: A Form of Love

The teacher of the family relations Sunday School class had invited class members to share memories of their own upbringing. "I think we can often learn a lot about how to raise our own children from the way we were raised. If any of you have recollections or comments about your own upbringing, I invite you to share those with us at this time."

Several people made statements about their youth: instances of love expressed in their homes, sacrifices made by parents for their children's good, discipline applied, and lessons taught. Then Brother Hunsaker raised his hand.

"I've thought of my folks many times over the years as we raised our own kids and enjoyed our grandchildren—of which we now have twenty-seven."

He smiled and shook his head slightly, as if surprised at the number, and went on. "I had wonderful parents who worked hard and always did their best for us kids. We were always busy. On a farm, there's always plenty to do. It seemed like we were always just barely getting by financially, as far as I could tell. But we never went hungry.

"In this class we've mentioned errors parents can make with their children, and I suppose we all experienced a few of those in growing up—just as we made our own when we became parents— though I think love overcomes a lot of those. But I do remember one thing that used to bother me a lot. I don't know if it was a parental mistake or whether I just needed something my parents couldn't supply." He glanced around as if wondering if he ought to continue.

"I don't think I've ever mentioned this to anyone, even to Wanda here, though we've been married now fifty-three years in March. It's just that I don't ever remember my folks ever really praising me or complimenting me. Not once do I recall . . ." The break in the old man's voice seemed to surprise him as much as it did the others in the class, who made quick sideways glances at him, then looked away, hoping he could go on.

He cleared his throat several times, loudly, and his wife put a wrinkled hand on his knee. He sniffed and tried to continue. "I'm sorry," he squeaked. His handkerchief came out of his pocket and he blew his nose.

"I shouldn't have started this . . . " At last, unable to say more, he arose and left the classroom. His wife sat stunned.

"I had no idea," she said lamely.

"Oh, now, that's just fine, Sister Hunsaker." The instructor seemed embarrassed. He was making an effort to go on to the next point of the lesson when the door opened and Brother Hunsaker stepped back into the room. All eyes turned toward him.

"I think I'd better finish what I started," he said. Standing by the door, he took a deep breath. "I really didn't know I still felt so deeply about this, but I remember very clearly as a young boy wanting to hear my dad say to me that I had done a good job. Oh, I know he appreciated the work we did, yet somehow I wanted to hear him say it. I wanted him to say, 'That was a good job, Elmo, of cleaning that ditch,' or 'You handle those cows well, son,' or something like that, just *anything*. I remember working extra hard on jobs and thinking ahead the whole time to what my dad might say to me, nearly begging for a compliment like that. But I never got one. Dad just wasn't the type." Brother Hunsaker had control of his emotions now and was speaking clearly, focusing on the window across the room. "I suppose it was silly to want that kind of praise. Why did I need it? I don't know. There were a lot of kids in our family, and maybe I just wanted to hear something that said I was special, to know I was really wanted.

"I love my folks dearly and I knew they loved me; they did the best they could." It sounded suddenly fierce. "And I don't want anybody to think anything bad about them. It's just that I never once heard them praise one of their children. And I'm sure that fact must have affected our whole lives and how we felt about ourselves."

Parents show love by providing a roof over their children's heads and food on their plates, by protecting them, teaching them, and helping them learn to make right choices, by preparing them in all ways to enter the world on their own. However, these parental contributions, vital though they are, can be perceived by children as quite removed and detached. They represent love of the broad, generalized type—love for humanity—as opposed to a narrow, specific appreciation for individuals, one at a time. And while love for humanity in the aggregate is wonderful and necessary, families need to provide specialized love for each family member.

The love that provides food, protection, and education typifies love in the remote sense—as in duties and legal obligations; the vital services it offers could as well be provided by governments, landlords, and teachers. Children require more. They need a more personal connection, one aspect of which is a need to be built up and helped to feel good about themselves as unique and irreplaceable human beings. Praise is a way of personalizing our love so our children know they aren't taken for granted, so they, as Brother Hunsaker says it, "hear something that said I was special, to know I was really wanted."

Children want and need parental approval, praise, and affirmation that they are doing well. Sometimes they will even crave such praise. And on those occasions, if they don't get it, they will assume they are not worthy. That assumption, though ill-founded, may harm their view of themselves for the rest of their lives.

In looking for sincere ways to give praise, parents can start with their children's accomplishments, no matter how small. In praising accomplishments, parents can do children an additional service if they will phrase their compliments in terms of "*You* must feel awfully good about . . . " or "Don't *you* feel proud of yourself when . . . " By this means, we show our children how to *praise themselves,* how to feel good about their own achievements so as not eventually to become too dependent on the praise of others to do a good job. They can thereby learn to achieve for the good feeling they create within themselves.

Children also need praise for *being* as much as for *doing,* so they don't come to think they're liked only when they're doing chores or working hard in school. They must know they're liked just because of who they are. Saying something like "Esther, I'm so glad you're in our family" is a start.

It may be a sad fact of life that most people don't get noticed for the things they want most to be noticed for. Yet we all have a right to be appreciated for *something,* and parents have many opportunities daily to help their children grow in the feeling that they are fine people.

To Be Trusted Is the Ultimate Compliment

"You don't believe me when I tell the truth.
Then next time, I'd just as well lie," said thirteen-year-old Nate, near tears.

"I didn't say I didn't believe you, Nate," said his mother. "I only want to be sure you always tell me the truth."

"How are you making sure of that? By asking me the same things over and over, hoping I'll mess up? I was at Jerry's house watching videos the whole time. And that's the last question I'm going to answer."

Nate stomped off to his room, leaving behind a damaged relationship and a mother knowing no more than she had before. Unfounded except in her own suspicions, her insinuations have only hurt her son's feelings.

"Then next time, I'd just as well lie." These bitter words indicate a child's certainty that he or she is not being believed, that his or her word is not accepted. Parents who interrogate or accuse without good reason—without actual evidence of deception—put a child in a very difficult position. Wrongly accused this time, the child may feel no reason to tell the truth in the future. In addition, if parental mistrust has gouged the child's self-image, lying may simply come easier next time. Since lying does sometimes appear to be the easy way out, and since people have doubts anyway, why, indeed, should a child bother to take the often more difficult route of telling the truth?

Parents must accuse only when they have reasonable evidence of wrongdoing. Interrogation seldom brings out information anyway. Even when evidence *is* available, a straightforward approach is best. If mom has called the home where her son is supposed to be watching videos and is told that the boys have left the house, she can begin by informing her son of what she's been told rather than by asking him leading questions that may back him into a corner.

When cornered, people instinctively defend themselves. And one form of defense is lying. If mom grills, "How *many* movies did you see?" "Did you see *all* of each of those?" "Did *anyone* leave the party?" she may cause her son to cover himself a little at a time until he's trapped and feels the need to make a bigger lie.

On the other hand, if mom comes right out and says what she knows, she gives her son a chance to tell her what happened. He may or may not be innocent, but he won't feel cornered, coerced, or tricked.

When parents trust their children, they clearly leave themselves open for the possibility of disappointment. But not trusting them—at least until they show reason not to—has a far greater potential cost. For the development of healthy self-esteem, children need to feel parental trust. Without it, they may come to feel there must be something wrong with them. And, like Nate, they may feel that, if they're going to be accused anyway, why not commit the deed?

Choices: Confidence-Builders

"How do you do it, Margaret?"

"Do what?"

"Raise such good children."

"Oh, you flatter me, Carol. What makes you ask me a question like that anyway?"

Margaret and Carol sat in the public observation deck at the city pool watching the swimmers below. Today was the final day of summer swimming lessons, and instead of their usual carpool rotation in driving their children to class, they had both come to view the tests and races.

"Margaret, I'm serious," Carol went on. "Your kids are always so well behaved; that's why I ask. Look at what's happening right now, for example. There's my nine-year-old down there acting like a six-year-old, splashing water and giggling instead of paying attention to the instructor. He's certain not to pass to the next level today. He won't work at anything. Right beside him is your boy, and he's paying attention, as he always does—in school, in church, in swimming lessons—doing perfectly what he's told. It's disgusting!"

Both women laughed, and Carol went on, "Look, we've been neighbors for years, our kids are all about the same ages, and I've always wanted to ask you your secret. I know you well enough to ask, don't I?"

"Well, sure, you can ask. But we have our problems, too, and I'm not sure my kids are any better than anyone else's," Margaret said.

"Then let me tell you how your kids are viewed in the neighborhood, compared to mine," Carol said. "You probably know that everybody raves about your family. All your kids are always so polite and respectful to adults. They've *never* been known to cause a problem for a teacher anywhere. In Scouts, the boys excel. In music lessons, your kids keep practicing and progressing. In church, they volunteer for talks and then do a wonderful job. They seem like angels to the rest of us."

Carol sighed. "Now, as for *my* kids . . . Mind you, I'm not trying to flatter you or make unfair comparisons. I love my kids, so don't get me wrong. And, of course, I would see their problems more than I would see anyone else's. But, even though people don't often tell me these things, I know my kids are seen as neighborhood menaces! They're noisy in church; they have no interest in music or even Scouts after the first couple of years; they generally refuse to work or help around the house; most of them won't give talks in church (the older ones sometimes refuse to even *go* to church); they cause problems at school. I know that the teachers dread seeing them on their class rolls in the fall.

"At times I feel like we're total failures as parents. We try to be democratic and let the kids have input into things, but that doesn't seem to have had the right effect. I sense that things are more structured at your house. Is structure your secret?"

"Structure is certainly a mark of our family," Margaret said. "Dan and I decided years ago that we would provide our children with a great deal of direction. I think most people would say we don't allow our kids many choices—or *any*. That sounds bad, I know, but Dan and I feel that kids need someone to give them direction and keep them busy. We're frankly not sure they can handle choices until they're grown.

"You mention music. There's an example. When we start our children on an instrument, we tell them they're not allowed to quit—simply not allowed. We think that helps them concentrate on the important things. In school, we expect the best and tell them so. If there's any slippage, we ground them or otherwise motivate them to do better.

"You say yours is a democratic home. I guess we don't really believe in democracy at our house," Margaret laughed. "When I see other people whose kids marry outside the church or don't go on missions, I really don't understand how parents can *allow* that. Maybe saying it this way is too strong, but I suppose we actually *force* our kids to do right. We make them choose the right when they're young so they will know how to do it when they're older. I won't let them make mistakes that will hurt them; I just won't! I don't know if our approach is right, though it seems to have produced good results so far. Of course, our kids are all still young, but none of them has ever really challenged us."

"Mine challenge me every day!" said Carol. "Maybe we've given ours so much freedom that they don't know how to handle it. They certainly don't seem to respond to anything except their own whims."

Carol and Margaret illustrate two extremes in child-rearing. Perhaps all of us know examples of each approach. The one is permissive; the other authoritative. Before we go further, let's hasten to point out that *neither of these approaches, as here depicted, is adequate.*

First, as to what Carol calls democracy, she's right about the defects of the approach as practiced in her home—her children have been given so little guidance and control that they don't know how to handle their freedom. They may enjoy a wide range of options; but with no guidance, their almost-random choices are frivolous and meaningless in terms of bringing them happiness now and in teaching them to make better choices in the future. They definitely need more parental support and family structure.

On the other hand, Margaret doesn't yet see the error of her ways, as serious as they are. This is generally the case with authoritative parents; their methods seem to "work" since their kids are outwardly as the parents want them to be: quiet, polite, respectful, obedient, easily controlled. What may not be seen until later—sometimes much later—is that such children may also be dull or frustrated or anxious, totally unable to make decisions on their own. Often their problems don't really surface until they are grown or nearly grown, at which point they start to have to make their own decisions and don't know how. At the worst, some of them come completely unglued—even as late as in middle age—when they realize they've never done anything because *they* wanted to; for all of their lives, they've done only what was expected of them. More than a few of them, at this point, have walked out on job, church, or family, largely because making the decision to do so—perhaps their first significant decision in life—was so powerful a feeling they couldn't resist it. Late-blooming independence often becomes rebellion, and it is much more dangerous than early childhood errors in making choices.

Neither approach is adequate. The one doesn't allow choices—necessary for growth and feelings of self-esteem—and the other doesn't give enough structure to make the choices meaningful and produce achievement—also ingredients of self-esteem. Children need guidance, but they also need choices—lots and lots of them, large ones and small ones—to practice on. They must also experience the consequences of their choices—unless too extreme or dangerous—to benefit from their practice.

A feeling of autonomy or self-direction seems to be basic to self-esteem, and childhood is the time to begin developing it. Wise parents will provide information, guidance, and help, but will leave as many decisions as possible to their children, who, as they mature, can assume ever more control over their own lives.

Past Decisions Are Best Left to Rest in Peace

Mrs. Sears and her married daughter were walking through the mall when they passed the piano and organ store. In the front display area sat a young salesman effortlessly playing an electronic organ.

"Oh, I wish . . . " Mrs. Sears began.

"Don't say it, mother."

"Say what, Val? How do you know what I was going to say?"

"I know exactly what you were going to say, mother. You've said the same thing for the last ten years every time someone plays a solo in church or a pianist is featured on TV or we walk past this store. 'Oh, I wish you hadn't stopped taking lessons, Val,' is what you were going to say."

Mrs. Sears's face flushed slightly. "Well, I do wish you'd kept up your piano. But I didn't know my feelings were so obvious. I guess it has been ten years since you quit your lessons, though, hasn't it?"

"Yes, mother, I was twelve, as you well know," Val said shortly.

"I'm sorry to have upset you, Val."

Val stopped and turned to face her mother. "Mother, think about it. How would you feel if you had been given a choice, told you could make a decision, and then, when you'd made it, been made to feel guilty for the next *ten years*! Well, that's exactly what you've done to me."

"Why, Val, I had no intention of making you feel guilty," her mother said, hurt in her voice. Val took her mother's arm and pulled her to a bench in the middle of the mall thoroughfare.

"Mother, I've bit my tongue for years, and I'll probably be sorry for not doing it again today, but I'm going to tell you how this has felt to me over all this time.

"As you know, I had taken piano lessons for three years, and I really didn't like piano very much. Maybe I was shortsighted, maybe I had more talent at music than I thought I did, maybe I would have come to like it better—all the things you told me. But the point is, you and dad gave me a choice—you told me to decide. I wasn't practicing and dad said he was wasting money on my lessons, and you said I had to choose.

"You said, 'You think about it, Val. You're twelve and old enough to decide for yourself.'

"So I thought about it. I thought hard about it. I realized I might be sorry if I quit because I'd always heard so many people say they were grateful to their parents for making them stick to their practicing. But I had tried and I simply did not like piano. So I announced my decision. I would quit.

"I felt so grown up that day. I had made a hard decision. I didn't take it lightly. I knew music meant a lot to you, and that you and daddy had spent a lot of money on my lessons already. But I was told I could decide, so I did."

Val paused for a breath and realized she'd been talking rather loudly and waving her hands. A couple of passersby showing obvious interest moved quickly on when she noticed them.

She lowered her voice. "And then, do you know what happened? Every day you'd ask me if I was sure of my decision. The next time we bumped into Mrs. Lasky in a store, you said, 'There's your piano teacher, Val. Are you sure you don't want to start

lessons again?' I said I was sure, yet you would find
a way to mention it at least once a week for the
next year, it seemed to me.

"I remember it was a whole year later when
Marge Johnson played a solo in church. You leaned
over and said, 'Marjorie is only a year older than
you, Val. You could have played that way.' And
still, after *ten whole years*, mother, you still can't
even pass a piano store without thinking—or saying—'Oh, I wish my daughter hadn't made such a
foolish decision.' "

By now, both women were near tears, one from
anger and the other from shock and hurt feelings.
"I'm sorry, mother. I was never going to mention
any of this. Now you know how I feel. What good
was it to tell me something was my decision if you
were not able to live with the result?

"And now that I've started on this, I felt the
same way about some of the other things you supposedly let me decide, like my not choosing to take
home ec, and about joining the ski club, and about
my going to Europe to study for the summer—and
by then I was twenty years old! You just have never
let anything rest." Val concluded, "And it all just
makes me feel that I must have been a very great
disappointment to you."

Is Val being unfair, too sensitive, or perhaps exaggerating her memories? Possibly. Young people are often insecure
enough about their decisions that they interpret an interested
party's simple interest as interference. It's clearly not out of
line for parents to ask if children might have changed their
view, especially after a passage of time or in light of new
information. Nor is it wrong for parents to want to protect
their children from the results of an impetuous decision made
beyond their experience. Still, it does appear that Mrs. Sears

has gone a bit far with her heavy sighs for what might have been.

Isn't a mother allowed to wish? Of course. But not out loud and not at the expense of her child's feelings. Val claims she was made to feel that her choice had inflicted a cruel and unnecessary injury on her mother—an accusation out of proportion to the size of the original issue.

The strong effect of parental reminders of past "mistakes" is apparent in the fact that, in spite of Val's certainty that her mother's approach is wrong, she still carries a feeling of guilt that, as a child, she failed her mother. Of course, young people who quit music lessons aren't really betraying their parents. Parents, however, can betray children's delicate self-esteem by continuing to remind them of what they "should have" decided.

Children do not turn out precisely as parents might dream. Though they will likely be delightful in ways parents never could have predicted, in other aspects they may be downright disappointments. But if they are to be anything at all, children must be themselves. After all the efforts of parents to infuse children with their views, children must make their own choices and their own mistakes. Standing back and letting their selections take them where they will may be the most difficult parental task of all, though perhaps the most necessary.

Labels Are Like Signs Around the Neck

Mr. Sands looked at Alison's list again. It wasn't a lot longer than most lists he'd received as a high-school counselor when he'd asked students with problems to list the labels they'd been given in their lives. The striking thing about Alison's list was that *none* of the labels was positive.

With a list like this, Mr. Sands felt he had a big clue to Alison's school and social behavior: "Fatty, nerd, cipher, four eyes, ugly, Miss Pudge, dummy, trash, crud face, slob."

He had simply said to her, "So I can get to know you better, and so you can perhaps better understand yourself, could you list for me several labels given you over the years? Some of these might come from many years back, but just list what you can remember, both positive and negative. You can list the positive ones on one side of the paper and the negative ones on the other. Now, take about five minutes and make your list."

Mr. Sands had asked hundreds of students over the years to make such a list. Only rarely had a student listed nothing but negative labels.

"Can you take a few more minutes and think of a few positive comments, Alison?" Mr. Sands asked gently.

Alison bent over her paper and chewed her pencil. But she could add nothing to her list. Mr. Sands feared that Alison faced a lifelong battle to overcome the labels hanging like millstones around her neck.

At the age of three, David was playing with his little friend, Jamie, from next door.

"Wet's go in the kitchen and get cake, David," said Jamie. "My mom's outside."

"Did she say we could?" David asked.

"No. She's outside. She can't see us."

"No. I have stwength," was David's reply.

Three-year-olds like David with an image of themselves as a person with "stwength" have a much better chance of success in life than teenagers like Alison who can't recall a single positive label. Even at the age of three, David had a view of himself that gave him power to make difficult decisions.

Of course, David wasn't born with this self-view. Somewhere—most likely from his parents—he gained the attitude that he could manage hard choices, just as Alison somewhere gained the concept that she was inferior, ugly, poor, and dumb. If parents can help children see strengths in themselves in the little things they encounter at home, then the inevitable peer attacks that come during the school years will have less effect. It's possible that it was not Alison's parents who actually gave her the negative labels, but they also may not have taken the trouble to fortify her against them in her formative years at home.

Going out of our way to label our children as strong, smart, cute, happy, friendly, and patient gives them a chance to incorporate these abilities into their lives as permanent qualities and to avoid the negative labels that will otherwise drag them down.

Self-Worth Is Not Connected with Fame and Recognition

How startled would a high-school graduate be on graduation day to pick up the local paper and read a paid announcement like the following:

We, the parents of this year's seniors at Danville High School, wish to take this opportunity to congratulate and publicly recommend the graduates to the world at large.

Not all of these students have achieved honors in school; most of them have not attained high scholastic rankings, and few of them have excelled in sports, music, or art. Only a handful have held positions in student government or titles of any kind; most of them are not presidents, editors, directors, or chairmen. Some have not belonged to school clubs or extracurricular organizations.

Those few who have excelled in these ways will be given special notice at graduation ceremonies. We are, of course, proud of their accomplishments too. However, in this space, it is those less spectacular achievers who will not be mentioned at the graduation ceremonies that we wish to recognize. This is our salute to the ordinary, average, standard students who tomorrow will go out into a world filled with mostly ordinary, average, standard people.

Two main traits stand out. We salute you for your gritty determination and perseverance, and for your basic humanity and goodness.

First, determination. Most of you have not found school easy. You've had to work hard to pass your classes. And you've learned to do so, to keep plugging away in spite of never being at the top of the class, of never being called forward at an awards assembly, of never seeing your name in the honor roll. The steady perseverance you have learned, the ability to work without praise or other external rewards—these will get you far in life. For most of life's work is of this kind—routine, steady, and basic, without obvious immediate reward. It's the kind of work that builds highways a foot at a time, sells groceries a can at a time, and teaches geometry a theorem at a time. Your perseverance is a character trait that will pay you rich dividends if you will carry this lesson with you: you can do what you have to do if you keep at it.

Second, your humanity and goodness. The qualities that make you good people now are those that will make you good spouses, parents, and citizens in the future.

No one will put your name in the paper because of the many little deeds you did to help other people along the way. But we have noticed, and we applaud you.

We've seen you go out of your way to speak to the shy, new student who seemed not to care that no one noticed him. You knew that, in spite of his reserved exterior, he was just like you inside. You knew he did care, and you cared enough to make him feel accepted.

We've seen you show concern in many other ways for the needs of others. We know of the service projects you carried out—collecting food for the needy at Thanksgiving, making Christmas decorations for the handicapped, organizing yourselves in church and school groups to clean the yards of widows, raising money for public library wheelchair ramps, taking up a collection for a classmate whose house burned, reading to the blind, learning sign language in order to communicate with the deaf, serving as auxiliary hospital aids, providing Christmas for less fortunate families, cooking breakfast at a shelter for the homeless, setting up fund-raisers to buy shoes for children in need, sponsoring a party for abused children, and acting as volunteers for the Special Olympics, to name a few.

We've seen your willingness to help your families through babysitting, sharing in household tasks, reducing the demands on the family budget by contributing to your own support through part-time jobs. Though most of you have undergone the usual spate of parent-youth discussions, arguments, and adjustments of growing up under parents who didn't always understand—or who understood too well—you've been a joy to your parents, who are very proud of you today.

You've shown yourselves in these and other ways to be the kind of good, decent, caring people who make the world a better place to live. This trait is vital. As you continue to show your concern for others—as you serve—you will find happiness for yourselves.

These two qualities—your basic goodness, along with your grit and determination—will bring you success and fulfillment, in spite of the inevitable difficulties and challenges the world will, to one degree or another, assuredly supply you over the years.

Graduation is a time for advice, and we feel there are two important concepts you need to keep foremost in mind as you leave the relatively sheltered halls of high school.

First, from our observations of the senior class, it's apparent that the world is a better place because you are in it. That's an important thing to know if you ever begin to suppose you aren't important because you aren't noticed by the world.

Be aware, therefore, that your personal worth is not connected to your public successes or fame. You are important because you are you, not because of what you can do or of what the world thinks of what you do. Most of your future work and good deeds may not be particularly noticed or applauded by the world. Continue them anyway.

The second important idea is this: High-school success is not a very important predictor of success in future life. It's true that there is life after high school. And this idea is critical for two groups of you. Those who were super-achievers in high school need to know this fact so you won't rest on your laurels. In spite of high-school success, you will yet have to prove yourselves again and again in the world. The other group, those who were average or below average in school, should take heart at this news too, for, in a few months or years, few will ask you what grade you got in algebra or whether *you remember the main points of the Magna Carta. You need to know that your main success in life can start right now and that you can still do great and important things. Being average is not a curse nor a failure. Being unrecognized by the world is not a problem. Yours is still the opportunity to do your best, to enjoy life, and to serve.*

Best wishes to you all.

Parents of the Senior Class

How easy it is for children to come to suppose that they are of real worth only if others say so—if, for example, they are cheerleaders, sports heroes, scholarship winners, or others in the spotlight. Although nearly all youth tend to walk to a greater or lesser degree by the reflected light of their peers, how much better if they can learn, sooner than later, to make their way by their own inner light. Those who do not learn it will eventually play upon a darkened stage as the school spotlight inevitably dims.

Parents who convey to their children that they are of value whether or not the world gives them acclaim will prepare them to work for the right reasons in the world. Wise parents will see that their children do not become overly enticed by the pied piper of peer fame, who leads them to dance to the fickle beat of fan applause rather than to the sweeter, inner chorus of self-direction, a music they themselves can turn on at any time.

Questions for Discussion

How do we rate the self-esteem of each of our children? Does any one of them need at the moment to be built up particularly? Do we have a long-term plan for creating high self-esteem in our children in the years they're in our home?

How are we at praising our children? Do we try to show them our love through compliments? Do we show them that they are appreciated just for being?

Do we trust our children? And do they know of our trust? Are we willing to trust them until they give us reason not to, even if that might mean we will occasionally put ourselves in a position to be deceived?

Do we allow our children to make choices? Do we allow them to experience the consequences of their choices, or are we constantly "saving" them from their choices, thereby canceling the learning effect?

Once a decision is made, do we accept it and not keep reminding our children of what might have been?

What kinds of labels are used in our home? Can we do more to put positive labels into our children's minds so they will see themselves in a better light?

Do our children know they can be good people without the attention of the world? Do they know that self-worth is not tied to how well they do any given thing nor in whether the world recognizes them?

4

Governing the Family

A child's first and most important lessons about how the world operates come through experiences with how the family is governed. The way a home is run conveys a great deal about parental priorities, desires, and goals. Some homes treat children as peripheral incompetents in need of constant direction; others make them the central feature, perhaps even letting them outrank mom and dad. Some families emphasize rules and order; others, freedom and self-determination.

To the degree that the home atmosphere is categorized by arbitrariness, bossiness, and excessive control, children grow up feeling that big people are authorized to direct all the affairs of shorter people. In such homes, instead of learning more about how to deal effectively with people, which is one of the main lessons home life should teach, children merely become anxious to get bigger so *they* can be in charge of someone.

However, parents can govern a family in a pleasant, democratic, consistent atmosphere, where relationships come before rules, where discipline is intelligent and reasonable, and where the positive is noticed, rewarded, and emphasized. Parents who pay attention to the little things, like those described in this chapter, have a better chance of raising children who know how to deal effectively and pleasantly with others and with life's many buffetings, large and small.

Family Democracy

"Whoa," dad said as the first child stood up from the dinner table. "Before everybody scatters, it's time we started discussing next summer's vacation. Let's clean up here and meet in the living room for a little discussion on that subject, shall we?"

Each person cleared his or her own table setting as ideas started to be generated.

"Seattle. That's where I want to go."

"No, San Francisco again."

It was dad's turn to clear the rest of the table and Dean's turn to wipe the table and counter. Ten-year-old Melanie rinsed dishes and started loading the dishwasher.

"If you want to leave those until we're through, we'll start now, Melanie," said mom.

In the living room, dad had the road atlas open to the western states. Mom started the discussion. "My major preference is that we somehow get to the Samson family reunion this year, either as a separate trip or as part of a bigger one. We've missed that for too many years now."

Several children seconded the idea.

Dad said, "I agree. What are some other ideas?"

"I want San Francisco," said Timmy. "I like the cable cars."

"We were there just last year," said Dean. "Why not Disneyland?"

All the smaller kids agreed with that.

"OK," said dad, "we're not ruling anything out, but remember that we were there two years ago and

that we haven't been to McArthur's in Seattle for
several years. We told them we would probably
come up this year. I'm not saying we have to, only
reminding us of what we once said we'd like to do."

"Yes, I want to go to McArthur's," Pete said.

"I think we've heard from everybody except
you, Lee," said dad. "What do you think?"

"I don't know." This was Lee's usual answer
lately. A moment's pause allowed him to add, "I
always wanted to go to South Dakota after I did a
report on Mt. Rushmore in the fifth grade."

"That's right," mom added. "We talked once of
taking that trip this year."

"We can't do that and see the ocean, too," said
Timmy. "I love the ocean. And the cable cars."

"Timmy," said dad, "we're not rejecting ideas
right now; we're only seeing what people think so
we can start to give it some thought. You're right
that we couldn't see everything in one trip. But
remember that last year we did go from San
Francisco clear down the coast to Los Angeles and
saw both areas in one trip. So some things can be
combined.

"Any other ideas for now?" dad asked.

Here is an example of family democracy in practice. Suggestions from all family members are easy to get if parents
set the stage for them and if children know their parents are
listening. Some parents fear giving their kids a vote because
they think adults must be "in charge" of every situation. At
times they might also fear that if their children are allowed
to make suggestions, they will be disappointed if their suggestions are not always taken. But children can learn that a
family can't do everything every member might suggest. The
majority will generally have to rule, although, in certain decisions, parents can't allow themselves to be outvoted by the
children. A family isn't a pure democracy where each vote is

equal. Like any organization, someone has to be in charge, and the majority vote will sometimes have to be overruled by parents.

The authoritative family, where family plans are made by pronouncement rather than listening and counsel, doesn't give children a chance to be involved. The permissive approach, on the other hand, permits the children to take over and become dictators. Neither of these approaches is much good.

Society has vacillated between authoritative and permissive approaches to child-rearing without realizing there was an altogether different approach. This alternative has been called the participative approach. It allows children to give suggestions and to be part of a democratic (not anarchic) family. It allows them to speak and to choose, yet it also provides structure, rules, and guidance to the extent needed for the ages of children involved. Participation allows people to express views and feelings and to be accepted for what they are. And it then teaches them to accept the wishes of the group.

Such a style is more difficult to manage and less efficient than parental dictatorship, but its rewards are much greater in terms of self-expression and family togetherness. Children's self-esteem is benefited in these families too—studies have shown that people with healthy self-esteems generally grew up in democratic homes.

Rules vs. Relationships

8:47 P.M.: "Arnold, I want you to be sure to get in bed on time tonight. This going to bed late has gone on long enough. You're ten years old and need your sleep."

(No answer.)

"Do you hear me?"

"Yes, mom, you say that every night."

"I mean it this time."

9:00 P.M.: "Arnold, it's 9:00. You haven't put away your models, and I don't think you're going to make it again tonight. Get to bed on time and you can read until 9:30."

"I will, mom."

"You'd better."

9:09 P.M.: "Arnold. Come in here."

"Yes, mom?"

"Your bedtime is 9:15. You've been late for weeks on end and I'm sick of it. Now get moving."

"I'm cleaning up now, mom. I have to get the glue put away or the baby will ruin everything tomorrow."

9:14 P.M.: "Arnold, it's 9:15."

"No, it isn't. It's only 9:14 on my clock."

9:15 P.M.: "Are you in bed?"

"Almost."

"Almost isn't good enough, Arnold. You get in bed right now. Right this second."

"In my clothes?"

"Don't get smart with me."

9:22 P.M.: "Arnold, why are you still up?"

"I'm just getting a drink. I'm in my pajamas. I have to get my clothes ready for tomorrow."

"Forget your clothes. Get in bed, right now."

9:31 P.M.: "Mom, did you sign my permission slip for the field trip?"

"Are you *still* up?!"

"No. I was in bed—I just got up to ask you about the field trip form."

"I'm not talking to you after 9:15."

"OK, just so I have everything ready for the field trip."

9:57 P.M.: "Arnold, why is your light still on?"

"I'm only reading. I'm in bed."
"You can't read until 10:00. You're only to read until 9:30. The light is going off."
"Just let me finish—Mom! Turn that light back on."

There is a definite problem here. We could talk about whose fault it is that Arnold doesn't get to bed on time and about inadequate communication. But the main issue is whether this scenario, repeated almost every night, does anyone in the house any good. Clearly a pattern has developed that is not healthy. Since Arnold knows he can get away with staying up, he endures the reminders to get what he wants, while the relationship with his mother suffers.

Sometimes rules get in the way of proper family relations. Certainly there's nothing wrong with established bedtimes and other rules that parents may require. It's the way they're handled that makes the difference. In this case, mom's relationship with her son is being damaged because she hasn't worked out a system of rewards and motivations—even punishments, if necessary—to get her boy to *put himself* to bed. He's plenty old enough to handle the matter.

A child in a situation like Arnold's can easily come to the conclusion that the only thing parents care about is the rules, when better handling could achieve the same results with virtually invisible rules. With shared responsibility rather than one-sided goading, parents are largely relieved of the constant reminding and the burden of enforcement—two of life's little things that can get in the way of the more important issues like having children enjoy being in their presence and feel like part of the family team.

Consistency vs. Arbitrariness

Dad was upset. Earlier in the evening, an encounter with his twelve-year-old son, Adam, over coming home from school on time, had not been

pleasant. Lately, Adam had made a habit of stopping at a friend's place without calling to ask permission. When dad had discussed this with him, the
boy had been a little defensive and unreasonable, so
dad had laid down the law—no TV tonight and no
more stopping at his friend's. The discussion left
dad angry about his son's attitude.

When Adam approached his dad on another
matter later in the evening, it was with some trepi-
dation.

"Dad, I want to sign up for community basketball this winter."

"Oh?" was the reply as dad turned down the TV.

"It's on Saturdays, starting in two weeks."

"How much does it cost?" dad asked.

"Fifteen dollars."

"I'll have to think about it," dad said.

"Well, I need to know," Adam pressed.

"I thought you said it started in two weeks.
What's the hurry?"

"Play starts in two weeks, but the last day for
sign-up is tomorrow," Adam said.

"Tomorrow? Why do you always wait until the
last minute? You know I need to talk these things
over with your mom, and we like time to think
about them."

"They didn't give out these papers in school
until yesterday—no, day before yesterday," Adam
protested weakly. "I forgot to bring mine home
until today."

"If you'd get home on time after school, maybe
there would be time to talk about these things," dad
attacked.

Now Adam was upset. "You're not here when I
get home anyway. You don't get off work until
later. So we couldn't talk then."

"Adam, I think we'll not sign up for basketball this year," dad concluded. "If I can't get better notice on something like this, then forget it."

Children can handle a great number of rules; they can stand chastisement; they can accept discipline; they can be told they can't do everything they might want to do. However, they have a strong sense of fairness. They know when "no" means more than no. When it means someone is upset with them in general or over something else, they find it hard to take because they know it isn't fair.

It must be pretty clear that dad, in this case, is being arbitrary. He's letting his feelings about his son's earlier behavior get in the way of his judgment on an unrelated issue. Although he has already punished Adam for coming home late from school, his decision not to let him enroll in basketball appears, whether dad knows it or not, to be an additional punishment for the same offense.

What dad needs to do now is say, "Let me think about it until morning." At that point he should be ready with a decision that bears only on the question at hand.

Tattling: To Tell or Not To Tell?

Mom was at the kitchen table studying her home-study course when six-year-old Jana ran into the room.

"Mom, mom, Leah's teasing me!" she yelled. "Make her stop."

Mom looked up from her work and calmly said, "Jana, I've told you not to tattle. You can solve this problem." She went back to her reading and ignored further protests from Jana, who soon went back to the family room to play with her older sister.

A few minutes later, sixteen-year-old Ann came into the kitchen. "Mom," she said, "I need to talk to you."

"What is it, Ann?"

"It's about Don. Maybe older brothers are supposed to know what they're doing and there might be no problem at all, but lately I've seen him going around with guys at school who have bad reputations."

"Oh?" Mom put down her book. "I think I'd better hear about what you've noticed."

An adult can see the difference in these two kinds of "tattle-telling." Kids can't always. Sometimes, in our efforts to teach our children to solve their own problems and not to become tattletales, we give them the impression that they are never to pass on negative information about anyone, anytime, for any reason. Teens, especially, usually have developed a strong peer-protection instinct. "It's their life," they say. "They can do what they want to. I wouldn't do it, but if others want to, that's their choice, and I would never rat on them."

A parent needs to make the point that there is a great difference in "ratting" on someone to get the person in trouble, and in watching out for people, in caring enough about them to get them help when they need it. Standard tattling gets people in trouble, whereas reporting to proper authorities gets help for people. Tattling is an act of retribution; reporting is an act of love.

Mom was right to listen to Ann but not to Jana. Now it's important for her to make sure her children know why she accepted one report and not the other so they can learn the difference.

In Defense of the Accused

Saturday lunch was finished and most of the family had left the table when mom decided to speak with James about his frequent raiding of the refrigerator.

"James, I think you've been getting into the doughnuts again. Am I right?"

"I had one the other day," James admitted. "And, I guess, I had one last night."

"I've told you before," mom said, "that desserts and special foods are off limits between meals. In a big family, people can't just help themselves to everything that looks good. A dozen doughnuts would be gone in five minutes if we all did that. And when I buy things like doughnuts, I freeze them for lunches and desserts."

"It's only once in a while," James protested.

Dad spoke up, "James, we've been over this before. It's not right for you to stake your claim to whatever you want when the other family members have to follow the rules. And it *isn't* just once in a while."

"He does it every day," Margo said. "Matt said he saw him eating a cinnamon roll this morning before breakfast."

"Those are my own!" James exclaimed. "I bought those."

"OK, James." Mom tried to restore peace. "We don't count those you buy yourself."

"I'll bet he didn't," said Margo, as she left the table.

"Stay out of this, Margo," said James. "It's not your problem."

"Ask Matt," Margo retorted. "He said he sees you eating things out of the freezer and the fridge all the time. Matt! Come in here."

"Now, just a minute . . . " mom began.

Dad spoke again, "You see the kind of reputation your sneaky behavior has created with your brothers and sisters, James. You talk like these things don't matter, but it's clear that others feel differently."

By now Matt was in the room. "James eats half of the desserts we have before the rest of us ever see them," he said.

James was now up from the table and near tears. "That's a lie. Mom, these guys don't even know that half the stuff I eat is my own. And people even get into *my* stuff sometimes!"

"Then you see how it feels, son," said dad unsympathetically.

"It's not fair," Margo added. "We all stay out of desserts, except James."

"Then who gets in *my* stuff?" James shouted.

"Hey, people, this discussion . . . " mom started.

"I'm out of this place," James said and he left the room.

Several mistakes are being made here. Even though James was obviously guilty of helping himself to more than his share of family sweets, he did not deserve the level of attack he received. What was the central mistake, other than mom's bringing up in the presence of others a matter best handled in private? Simply that the prosecution became persecution because too many people were allowed to join the bombardment. Although some of the accusations were less than accurate, since part of what he ate was his own purchase, James still went away feeling attacked by the whole family.

There are two rules about discipline parents would do well to enforce. First, when a child is being reprimanded, his or her brothers and sisters are to stay out of it entirely. Ideally, they should not even be present. Certainly they should not be allowed to assist in the siege. If they have pertinent information, they might be called in later or one at a time. Second, generally speaking, one parent at a time ought to be sufficient as prosecuting attorney. The other can act as a neutral party or even a public defender to keep the level of the charges and the emotions down to a reasonable level. Otherwise, a minor incident can escalate into full-scale warfare. Two parents down on a child at one time simply provide too much intensity for a young person to handle.

All children make mistakes and all children need correction. But often their side of the story alleviates the charges somewhat, and that side of the story must always be heard. Otherwise, without a chance to express their views and with everybody in town pointing fingers, what starts out as a minor infraction comes across to children as major and very unfair. Even the accused—*especially* the accused—need friends.

Discipline: Helpful or Harmful?

It would have been much better for three particular boys to have gone to Sunday School class after priesthood meeting than to have slipped out the back door of the church to see how well the falling snow would pack. But twelve-year-olds (like the rest of us) don't always have the foresight to know what's best for them. By the time the Sunday School presidency was apprised of their absence, they had found that the new snow packed very well indeed and that a few of their snowballs could reach all the way to the main road. By hiding behind cars in the parking lot, the boys could glimpse the reactions on the faces of the startled drivers whose cars were smacked in the side by the heavy white missiles.

When Brother Houton of the presidency learned that among the missing from course 12 was his boy Scott, he figured Art Bigler and Kyle Cheney would almost certainly be the other two with him. The three were nearly inseparable. The teacher confirmed this suspicion. The boys didn't seem to be anywhere in the building, but when an irate driver stopped by the bishop's office to report that his car had been hit by a snowball, Brother Houton knew where to look.

"Joe, let's find our boys," he said to Joe Bigler, Art's dad, who, as an assistant clerk, was working at the moment on membership records in the bishop's office.

"Oh, is Art one of those renegades throwing snowballs?" Joe asked as he stood. He was a big man, over six feet tall and with a build that could have qualified him as an AFL lineman. The angry look in Joe's eye made Brother Houton wonder if he'd made a mistake in asking him to come along. He didn't want an unnecessary uproar; he only wanted to get the boys to class.

By the time the two men reached the back door of the building, the boys were on their way back in to rejoin their Sunday School class and regain a bit of the warmth of the Spirit, having had all the winter sport their red hands could stand for the time being. But at that moment, ten-year-old Charlene Carter, who had remembered her scriptures in the family car and come out to retrieve them, started up the sidewalk, seemingly unaware of the boys. Such a cute and demure target was simply too much temptation to resist. Simultaneously, six hands reached to scoop up snow to toss in her direction.

The attack was really nearly harmless; one scoop came nowhere close, another only brushed the hem of her dress, and the third never got thrown at all because two things happened suddenly and simultaneously. First, pushing open the glass doors, Joe Bigler shouted "Stop that!" and, second, Charlene made a little sideways hop—either because of the shout or because of the thrown snow—and dropped her Triple Combination into a small puddle of very muddy water. It sank upside down, right up to Alma, chapter 28.

Everyone froze in place. Charlene issued a low "Oh," and stared down at the book. The first to thaw out was Kyle Cheney, who moved on up the sidewalk in slow motion and into the building, muttering, "We were just going to class," as he passed Brother Houton and Brother Bigler.

Charlene was next to move. She bent over and picked up her dripping book, turned to the two remaining boys, and hissed, "Idiots. It was new." In unison the boys replied, "Sorry." Charlene held the muddy book at arm's length and went into the building.

Joe Bigler suddenly rushed toward his son, his arms outstretched as if preparing to sack an opposing quarterback. But when he reached Art, both his huge hands came down on top of his head. Art looked confused. Was this to be a father's blessing?

It was not. Art's mouth twisted in pain as he felt himself being lifted by the hair straight off the ground. But other than his sharp, startled intake of breath, Art made no sound. When he was lowered to the ground, tears were running down both cheeks.

"Now, get home," Joe bellowed. "I'll deal with you later."

Scott Houton looked at his friend in horror as the boy scurried across the slushy parking lot, head hanging down. Brother Houton didn't know what to say. He managed, "Scott, I think you'd better get to class." Scott hurried in, leaving the two men silent in the falling snow.

Discipline is tough to handle. Few parental responsibilities are more difficult. However, there are clear principles of correct discipline. One is that it mustn't hurt the spirit. It mustn't embarrass or cut children down in front of friends. It must be just, fair, appropriate to the level of the infraction. Ideally, discipline is a teaching tool, not a punishment.

Both Art and Scott needed disciplining. Art received his swiftly and cruelly. Scott will face his when he gets home after church, although he has already learned that even the innocent fun of youth can sometimes turn into trouble. By then, he may even be ready to volunteer to replace Charlene's ruined scriptures. And he will very likely accept his dad's suggestion to collect a third of the cost from each of the other boys.

For Scott, this experience may turn out to be a valuable learning experience. What Art learns may be much different and much less positive.

Obedience: An End in Itself?

"I'll have to admit, that was a great party," Al said as he turned the car onto the highway toward home.

This was a significant statement coming from Al, who did not like parties on principle. "I thought you'd enjoy the Williamsons. I've found her so interesting at work," said Pat. "Weren't their kids great singers? I wish we could get ours to do something like that."

"Oh, yeah, they were very good, right down to the littlest one. What was he, about three or four?"

"Tommy is three. Connie has told me all about him," Pat said. "And all five of them were so well-behaved, too."

"I suppose they spend a lot of time practicing," Al said. "That would be the tough part."

"Oh, yes, I know they do," Pat said.

They drove in silence for a few moments. Then Al said, "You know, there was something about those kids that bothered me a little, though."

"Oh? What was that?" asked Pat.

"I don't really know what to call it," Al said. "They seemed . . . well, almost too well-behaved. I know that sounds dumb considering how often I try to get our kids to shape up. Still, those kids were just too controlled—maybe that's it. Like they didn't dare do anything without looking at Connie or Jack to see if it was all right. Did you notice it at all or did I see more than was there?"

"Well, I did see a little of that. I thought maybe they were just shy around the group. But now that you mention it, Connie has said they are quite strict parents. They expect a lot from their kids. And I guess Jack is very stern with them, Connie says, always correcting how they speak and so on. He also expects absolute obedience at all times."

"When I really noticed it was when the little one made that little hiccup or whatever right before they started to sing, remember?"

"Yes, that was funny."

"Well, the next older child, the blond girl, started to laugh, along with the rest of us. The older kids didn't, I noticed, but she started to, then she glanced at her dad. I didn't see his face, but I saw hers. She stopped laughing instantly, and I saw what I would call fear in her eyes. And then the way they all marched straight up to bed right after they sang, without even glancing at the candy bowl or getting a drink of the punch that was right there, even when people invited them. The whole thing didn't seem quite natural to me."

Absolute obedience at all times. How wonderful it sounds to the typical parent, frustrated at times by his children's willfulness. Yet surely no one would think that immediate, invariable, and unquestioning obedience wouldn't carry with it large problems of its own.

Obedience is easily overrated. A great control mechanism, it is not a virtue in itself. It's neutral. Like faith, obedience makes sense only when connected with something else. By itself, it has no direction or purpose. In the abstract—without a connection to someone or something positive—it can as easily lead people to unquestioningly follow a Hitler as a Messiah. Obedience has value when attached to following the good, and that implies choice, not blind submission.

It could even be argued that obedience in children isn't natural. A child's natural instinct is to explore and question and strike out on his own. Not that some instincts can't bear restraining. But demanding absolute submission is going too far the other way. Children reared under such a system grow up either beaten down (if they give up their instincts to explore life on their own) or evasive and guilt-ridden (if they pretend to give up yet continue a clandestine disobedience).

One problem with excessive parental demand for obedience is that it is not easily outgrown—by parent or child. When are children expected to grow out of submissiveness and make their own decisions? At fifteen? At twenty-five? Do we want twenty-five-year-olds afraid to breathe without mother's permission? If, instead of demanding kowtowing, parents can teach the "whys," perhaps their children can learn to be cautious, wise, and trusting without the need for something as unnatural and stifling as resigned passivity.

Parents: Servants or Slaves?

Look, Dick. Look, Jane. Look, look. See mother run. Mother is very busy. Look at Friday's schedule in mother's planning book:
    6:30   wake up Jeri

6:45   make five lunches

7:10   wake up Cliff

7:15   wake up Paul

7:30   wake up JoAnn and Karlene

7:35   drive Jeri and Cliff and friends to high school

7:50   drive Paul to junior high if he misses the bus again

8:15   drive JoAnn and Karlene to elementary school

9:00-10:30   type Jeri's paper and deliver to school

10:30   drive Karlene's overdue library book to school and pay the fine

11:00-12:30   make cupcakes for Cliff's party

2:00-3:00   pick up videos and refreshments for Cliff's party

3:15   pick up JoAnn and Karlene from school

3:30-4:00   drive JoAnn to piano lesson

4:45-5:30   drive Paul on paper route

6:30-7:15   set up family room for Cliff's party

7:30   drive Paul to sleep-over

8:30-10:30   serve at Cliff's party

10:30-11:30   clean up after Cliff's party

Some parents might find such a schedule routine. To most of us, it appears a heavy—unnecessarily heavy—schedule. Parents ought to help their children, ought to make available to them opportunities and activities, ought to be leaders who are willing to serve. But serving is not to be confused with slavery.

The facts in this case are that alarm clocks are readily available in the stores; the high school and the elementary schools are no more than several blocks away; the children are all able-bodied and have shoes on their feet; Jeri, a senior, knows how to type; JoAnn's piano teacher lives six blocks away; and Paul's paper route lies in an area of five square blocks only a half-mile from home. With these facts, a mother with a schedule like this has taken upon herself a load of responsibility for her children's chores more appropriate to a slave. Not only is this pattern excessively demanding of mother, who ought to have a chance for a life of her own, but it is also, in the long run, probably harmful to the children.

Children can learn to take responsibility for those small and large matters in their own lives that will help them develop into responsible adults. Returning their own library books, typing their own papers, getting themselves out of bed, catching the bus, and doing most of the planning and work for their own activities and parties are things that young people can handle. If mother *wants* to help to some degree, that's fine. The problems come when she thinks she has no choice and when the children expect and demand it.

Some parents need too much to be needed. Parents ought, more reasonably, to teach their children to be responsible and then make themselves available in the background to help when there are special needs.

Nagging: The Most Annoying Parental Trait

Marsha was on the phone with a friend from up the street. "Yes," she said, "Andrew finally got his Eagle in Scouting. I almost feel like saying 'I got an Eagle in Scouting.' "

Marsha sighed and sat down on the couch. "Andrew was ready for his Eagle at thirteen; he'd done virtually everything except plan and complete the big Eagle project itself. He didn't seem to find a project he liked, and we didn't push it. Dan and I thought he had plenty of time and that it would be better to let him come to it on his own, you know, and not feel pushed.

"But when he turned seventeen and still couldn't organize himself enough to get going, I decided to

start pushing. I decided I would ask him about it—
just reminders, you know, to show interest—every
chance I got. I didn't want to make a pest of myself
and have him rebel and turn against the whole idea.
However, I started asking him about it every day.

"I came up with project ideas, and then I'd ask
him 'Andrew, have you called the Forest Service
about which trails to mark?' 'Have you talked to
your Scout coach, Andrew?' and so forth. I didn't
let up. At last, he finally got it done. I think he's
very glad. He's got a buddy downstairs right now
looking at his award, in fact. I don't think he even
realizes I guided him as much as I did."

Meanwhile, downstairs in Andrew's room, a
slightly different conversation was occurring.

"So you finally did it, Andy. Got your Eagle, I
mean."

"Oh, yeah, I got it. I had no choice."

"What do you mean?

"Burt, you don't have a mom like mine or you
wouldn't have to ask. She drove me nuts. Talk
about nag! Starting about three months ago, she
started asking me every twenty minutes day and
night how I was doing on my Eagle. So I started to
call around about different projects, but I couldn't
find anything really good. Finally, I got fed up and
decided I wouldn't get it at all.

"Then when I told the coach I wasn't going to
get it, he asked me why. I told him my mom was
driving me crazy. And he convinced me to ignore it
and not let that keep me from doing what I knew I
would be proud of later. So I decided to go ahead
and do it. I chose a stupid project I didn't want to
do, just to get mom off my case."

Did Marsha do the right thing? It's hard to say. Her boy
has his Eagle, and he may feel proud of it in the future. Right

now, he doesn't seem to. He seems to feel only relief to get out from under the pressure. Marsha is clearly wrong about how her "reminders" and "showing interest" affected Andrew. He called it by its right term, "nagging."

Nagging can have a tremendously negative effect. It tells a child that parents run his or her life, that they are dissatisfied with the present course of things, and that they won't let up until they get things the way they want them. Sometimes, if nagging goes on for too long a time, it becomes the primary way two people relate. One person becomes dominant and the other resentful, guilty, and anxious to avoid contact. That's a pretty heavy cost. Parents need to weigh this carefully. There is always a better way to show interest.

The Positive Is Harder to Notice Than the Negative

"Alysa, your room is a disaster." Dad stood in the doorway looking at the clothes, books, and toys on the floor. "Why can't you keep this place clean?"

"I do sometimes, dad," Alysa replied. "But you never notice when I do."

"Oh?" Dad sensed he might be walking into a trap but saw no way out. "And when was it last clean? Last summer?"

"Last weekend, for both days, I made sure there was *nothing* left on the floor at all. I waited for you to say something, but you never did."

How easily parents notice the negative, and how often they miss the positive. This can be very discouraging to children. They often try so hard to please that parents' failure to notice the good can be very disappointing to them, and it's also one of the least effective teaching tools anyone could devise. Children generally respond much better to parents' observations of improvement than to just another complaint.

Noticing just one improvement is a little thing, yet it will often do more to produce better behavior than a week of harping on the blunders.

Questions for Discussion

How do we feel about democracy in our family? Is it actively being taught in our home? How could we better indicate to our children that we are willing to hear their ideas and concerns?

Recognizing that rules are clearly necessary, are there rules in our home that get in the way of our relationships with our children? Are we certain the rules are worth the cost? How can we let our children know we value relationships more than rules?

Would our children rate us as consistent or arbitrary? How can we be careful to be more fair and consistent?

Do our children know the difference between tattling for bad reasons (to get someone else in trouble) and for good reasons (to help someone)?

Do we take steps to keep the family from ganging up on the one accused when a problem is being discussed? Can we make sure one parent acts as a neutral party or a defender in these discussions?

How can we work to achieve discipline that is basically helpful rather than hurtful?

How do we view the need for obedience in our children? Do we believe obedience is an absolute or merely a neutral guideline until attached to someone or something?

Are we slaves to our children? If so, is this the role we want to be in? Is our role helpful to the children in the long run?

Are we naggers? How can we better communicate interest without the negative effects of nagging?

Do we notice the positive in our children? Do we go out of our way to let them know we've noticed?

If we choose to make changes in these areas, can we foresee some of the problems that might occur and work out contingencies and solutions in advance?

5
Family Communication

Few things are more necessary in a family than proper communication—honest, straightforward, nonmanipulative, understanding—with an attitude of loving acceptance and problem-solving. While most parents give open communication a nodding acceptance, many either don't feel comfortable using it or don't know how to actually apply it.

A great number of adults were handicapped as youth by growing up under parents who neither understood nor valued the expression of feelings. Generations lived under the mistaken notion that mature people always kept their feelings to themselves, showed no emotions, and waited problems out. Particularly was this image applied to males, who were to be macho, cool, and aloof from emotional intensities.

Fortunately, these views are changing, and most people have embraced to some degree the idea that saying what they feel is healthy—not when it will hurt others, of course, but when it clears the air, moves people toward better understanding, and opens the way for solutions to problems that may otherwise build up for years.

Many of the little things parents do in the home either contribute toward a closed atmosphere, where people walk around in their own emotional cocoons, unable or unwilling to allow others into their hearts, or toward openness, where love and trust encourage honest expression. Parents who opt for the latter will raise more emotionally healthy children, as illustrated in both positive and negative ways in the following examples.

Complaining vs. Discussing

It was a typical Sunday dinner-table discussion. The Haskins generally had a lively commentary on news events, politics, and issues of the day, and the children were always encouraged to participate. After a discussion of a particular bill under debate in Congress, seven-year-old Sarah, who seldom had much to say on these matters that were a bit over her head, made a startling comment.

"Our country is in awful bad shape, isn't it, dad?"

Such a serious comment, coming from the mouth of his happy second-grader, left dad speechless for a moment. Finally, he asked, "What do you mean, Sarah? Where did you hear that?"

"Why, from you, dad," Sarah replied, "You say bad things about the government all the time."

Dad was dumbstruck. "I do?" he managed. "I . . . I can't think what you mean."

Now Sarah was embarrassed. "Oh, I don't know," she said.

Later, after most of the family had been excused, dad said, "I'm amazed at what Sarah said. What do you suppose she could mean?"

"I think I know," his wife said. "I believe we sometimes get involved in a discussion with one another or with the teenagers and we forget how the little ones can interpret things. For example, a few weeks ago, Sarah said to me, 'Isn't Joey's mom going to go to church anymore?'

"I asked what on earth gave her that idea, and she said she had heard Jolene and me talking about a problem she was having in her Primary calling. I hardly even remembered the conversation, but then I recalled one day when Jolene brought Joey to play, we got to talking about Primary matters, and she told of her frustrations with her new class. It was really nothing much—she was just *talking*. I guess Sarah must have taken it seriously. I was as shocked then as you are now."

"But I haven't done that, have I?"

"There's little I can remember specifically, and certainly nothing that would have upset an adult. Still, we've been talking about the economy and unemployment and all kinds of problems lately. And you did say one night at dinner—maybe for the sake of argument—that you didn't see how things could go on without major changes. I suspect we've made slurs about certain politicians, too, that might come across as pretty heavy to a seven-year-old."

The Haskins are discovering that there are different levels of conversation and meanings. Adults may make statements that are understood in context by other adults but that might have no context whatever to a child. To another adult, a statement like "Isn't it sad what a mess Congress is in" might not mean anything more than disapproval of a particular item under consideration. It's hardly a call to revolution. Yet, to a child, a comment like this, without further explanation, might sound very serious and frightening indeed.

The most patriotic citizens have sometimes made statements about the country that, taken singly and out of context, could be called seditious! In addition, people sometimes make comments about Church programs and leaders as well as educational policies and local government matters that might sound stronger than they were meant to be.

Children need to learn the difference between discussing and complaining. They can come to value the freedom of speech we enjoy in our country, not as an opportunity for useless carping, but as a precious chance to think, speak, and discuss in intelligent ways, even when people differ.

Long live dinner-table discussions, one of the most important "little things" parents can foster. Still, we must be careful about the strength of our statements and the possibilities of misinterpretation. When younger children are deliberately brought into the discussion, even when their views are not as well formed or as well stated as those of older children, parents will learn how the younger ones are interpreting the conversation.

Openness and Willingness to Talk About People

It was 7:30 P.M., time for Mara to be getting home from work. Mom had kept dinner warm as usual. At sixteen, Mara had her first part-time job, working for her uncle Will, her mom's brother, at his fast-foods spot in the mall. After only a few weeks, Mara was showing signs of being upset about the job. She didn't seem to agree with a lot of Will's decisions, and she resented his style of management, which she called "bossy."

Mom heard the car in the driveway. The intensity with which the door from the garage shut—not quite a slam but almost—told mom that Mara was upset again. After a few minutes in her room, Mara came to the living room.

"Hi, dear," mom said, "I have your dinner ready."

"I'm not hungry," Mara said quickly. "Mom, I can't work for that man."

"Oh."

"Mom, before I went to work for him, I had no idea Uncle Will was such a . . . a *tyrant!* You ought to see him at work. He thinks he's a little Napoleon or something. He watches us girls like he can't wait to see one of us put a fraction too much mustard on a hot dog. I'm new, so I expect him to worry about me. But one girl has been there three years, and he still gets on her like crazy. She's about to quit. Nobody else has ever lasted even that long. I think he's sick."

Now mom was aroused. "Mara, I won't have you talking about your uncle that way. He's run his business for years and done well, and I'm sure he knows what he's doing. If you can't handle it, you can quit, I guess. But if you can't say something nice about people, especially your relatives, I don't want to hear it."

Here is a case of wrenching an adage to the point of breaking it. "If you can't say anything nice . . . " has guiding value as a means of curbing useless, harmful, busybody-type gossip. If we try to make it a replacement for meaningful discussion and problem-solving, it becomes nonsense.

People do get upset with others and encounter behaviors they don't understand. Being unable to mention their concerns to anyone because of a misapplied aphorism is frustrating and leaves them not knowing how to cope. While Mara might be overstating the problem, approaching it in an immature manner, and seeing only one side of it, the matter is still of genuine concern to her.

What her mother fails to perceive is that Mara's statements need not be viewed as a criticism as much as a request for help. When adults turn a deaf ear to concerns because they are not phrased in acceptable ways, they do a great disservice to children. Mom has missed an opportunity to understand how Uncle Will comes across at work and what might be done to help her daughter cope with the situation. Telling people they shouldn't feel a certain way or shouldn't express it if they do is telling them how they are allowed to think and feel, something no one is authorized to do.

Talking about people has been classified as gossip. Only little minds talk about people, we're told. But nothing is more interesting than people. And by talking about them (not belittling or hurting them—*that's* gossip), by recognizing and discussing their traits, whether good or bad—our children have a better chance of understanding others and themselves.

Compromise: A Vital Skill

Dad had cornered his daughter in the kitchen one morning. "I don't see why you can't get your chores done, Angela," he said. "We've talked about this problem so many times, but nothing ever seems to change. Last night's dishes are still in the sink, and yesterday was your day for kitchen duty. And now you go off to school and we have nothing to eat on unless someone else does your job."

"I didn't have any time last night. I didn't even eat here, dad. It doesn't seem fair."

"You didn't eat here, but it's still your day for dishes. Why couldn't you do them when you got home from the church party?"

"Well, it was 10:30, and I still had homework. I didn't get to bed until 12:15. By then I was wiped out."

"I don't know what to do about it. We all have hard days. These dishes will be waiting for you when you get home from school, and in the future, you'll have to do your chores on the day they're due, even at midnight."

Perhaps dad's response is reasonable. He may be trying to teach Angela that responsibilities have to be met in spite of parties and homework. That isn't a bad lesson. Without it, youth learn to use these and other excuses rather well.

But why couldn't some other arrangement be made for Angela to help her get the work done? If dad is right that this problem has occurred "many times," isn't it time to find a solution?

What about a compromise? Perhaps the conversation could have gone differently.

When dad said, "I don't know what to do about it," he might have added, "But maybe we should explore what can be done. Are you willing to discuss other options for your share of the work?"

"Yes, I'm willing, dad."

"There are days that are very busy for you, what with volleyball at church and your homework load this year. Maybe there are particular days we should avoid entirely for chores at home. Are there certain days that are always bad?"

"Thursday is usually the worst. I have an extra lab after school and then I have volleyball—at least during the winter. Tuesday is nearly as bad because of the volleyball, except I don't have the lab."

"I think we could avoid assigning you chores on those two days. The other kids could fill in then and you could do more on other days. Would that help?"

"Yes, it would."

"Also, maybe it's time to look at the whole chore chart to see about some realignment. With the heavier school schedule you have now that you're in high school, maybe we need to give you the type of chores that could mostly be done on Saturdays rather than those that require daily assignments. I'll look at that question with mom and we'll see what we can draw up. You have to go now, so let's talk again tonight."

"Thanks, dad."

Some people don't believe in compromise. "When you're right, you're right," they say. They live in a world that most of us don't live in, where issues are only black and white. They can't see that most of our activities don't fall into the extreme categories of eternal truths or evil falsehoods.

To most parents, compromise is not a bad word. While perhaps some things can't be altered, most can. It may take a little more effort, yet when parents show their willingness to compromise, they indicate an interest in working with their children, in bending to fit their needs where possible. Children then know their parents care more about them than about preconceived absolutes.

Parents who refuse to compromise in their dealings with their children teach quite another lesson and exert considerable needless pressure on them in things like chores and school expectations, when a little understanding could go a long way.

Parents Must Not Radiate Hostility

An excerpt from Leslie's journal at age nine:
Mom seems mad at me all the time. She told me
I was selfish with my sisters.

Leslie's journal at age fifteen:
I feel like I've never done anything to please my
mother. I don't really care anymore, but I feel
funny about it sometimes. She's cool to me almost
all the time, it seems to me. Once in a while she's
OK, but I can expect it to change back to anger
soon. And it always does. She doesn't like some of
my friends, and maybe this is her way of showing it.
I know mothers love their kids, but love and
like aren't the same thing, and I'm sure my mom
doesn't like me.

Leslie's journal at age eighteen:

We had a mother/daughter luncheon at church, and each girl was supposed to say something nice about their mom. Jo said hers was her best friend. Nan said her mother was a person she could always talk to. Then it was my turn, and I had to say something. I could only say my mom was a good cook.

It seemed so dumb not to be able to honestly say good things about her. I do love her, but I have never felt close to her. For as long as I can remember, she always has seemed disapproving of me.

Maybe I'm exaggerating the problem. I know mom loves me, and she's done a lot for me. Sometimes she even seems to value me as a person, but most of the time, that's not so clear. She'll get upset about something—dating or something—and she'll be cool toward me for weeks.

It's probably my fault. I don't know. Maybe I expect too much, although my friends, most of them, seem to have a better feeling about their moms.

Here is a major problem, and blaming it all on mom would be extremely unfair. Let's face the fact that some children are easier to get to know and be close to than others. Still, there is a troublesome characteristic in her mother that Leslie, by age eighteen, has correctly identified: she uses a mild hostility to indicate disapproval.

Mother herself would describe her behavior this way: "When my children are in a pattern of poor behavior, I show them my disapproval to keep them reminded of how they ought to live. For instance, when Leslie was nine, I talked to her about her selfishness. When she was fifteen, she was going with a bad crowd and I had to keep her reminded of that. At eighteen, she was doing pretty well, yet there were times when she would stay out late and think more of boyfriends than of schoolwork. All of these were typical, I suppose, for the age—but I didn't want to just let them go. I wanted her to know I disapproved of her life in those ways."

What mother doesn't see is that her way of "reminding" Leslie of her behavior doesn't work. Leslie often doesn't even know the problem mom has in mind, so all she feels is rejection. And, even if not intended to the degree Leslie feels it, rejection will negatively affect her whole life.

Parents are authorized and expected to tell their children what they dislike in their behavior and work out plans for improvement, but they must not continue to radiate disapproval and rejection.

Feelings Are Better Expressed Than Buried

Marilee knew she'd have to find a good time to talk with her husband if her comments were to be accepted. Finally, on Sunday afternoon, when the house was quiet and Charles had finished reading the paper, she approached him in the living room.

"Charles, I want to talk to you about something."

"OK. Go ahead," Charles said.

"Well, it's hard to bring up things without sounding like I'm blaming you, and I'm not." Marilee was nervous. She knew starting would be the hardest part. "It's about the way you deal with the kids sometimes."

"Oh, that," Charles sneered. "We've been over this before."

"Yes, I know we've started to talk about it before, Charles, though I don't feel we've ever really talked it through. And I certainly don't feel anything has changed."

"No, and I don't suppose it will. Just because you let the kids get away with murder, you think I'm too strict when I discipline them at all. I can't change what I think is right. We were raised differently, Marilee."

Marilee sensed Charles's controlled anger. She fought to keep her voice calm when she said, "I understand that's how you see it—that I'm lenient and you're the one who handles the kids in the right way—but I wish we could sit down and talk through the implications of both ways. I'm certainly not saying I'm right and you're wrong—"

"Oh, yes, that's exactly what you've always said." Charles's clipped words indicated his rage. His voice took on a kind of sarcastic singsong effect when he was irritated. But he never let himself admit anger or other emotion. How Marilee would have preferred him to shout and throw things than to take an aloof stance that said he was above these feelings.

"No, Charles, that isn't it. I've never said that." Marilee chose her words very carefully to avoid blaming Charles.

"But lately, some of the children, now that they're older, have expressed feelings of your rejecting them when . . . "

"Oh, so they come to you to save them from me, huh? And you listen to all of it. Well, that's just great." Charles pasted on a wry and fake smile that narrowed his eyes. "If my own kids have to go bawling to their mommy about me, I don't want to hear about it. You know I can't stand their feeling sorry for themselves. And you, every time we talk, you do the same thing. If you think you can get me riled over your petty emotional issues, that won't happen." He slowly turned in the swivel rocker toward the window.

"Charles, all I'm saying—"

"I said I don't want to hear about it, Marilee."

The room was silent for several moments. Marilee had vowed she would not cry this time, but she did.

At the sound, Charles got up and left the room. "You know I can't stand sniveling," he said. "I want you to understand I'm willing to discuss things, but only on a mature level."

Let's leave this painful scene as fast as possible. At the risk of oversimplification, maybe we can analyze the problem. We don't want to place all the blame on one party, but obviously Charles doesn't accept criticism gracefully. However, there's more to the situation: Charles doesn't accept *feelings*. He hasn't yet heard Marilee's specific concerns or criticisms, yet he makes it clear from the start that he doesn't want to hear them, even before he hits upon the convenient excuse that he doesn't like "sniveling."

Most of all, as shown by his rejection of Marilee's new information about the children, by his imposed control on his own anger, and by his departure from the room, Charles makes clear that he doesn't want to show *his* feelings. In spite of his departure statement about his implied maturity, Charles does not want to endanger his sense of control by discussing the matter.

While this case may seem extreme, it is not terribly unusual, and lesser versions abound. People like Charles protect themselves through their aloofness and refusal to participate. They maintain control of their family through their rejection of alternate views, even when those views could improve the situation immensely. The effect on their spouses and children is often devastating, particularly if these family members desire a more honest approach and are left with no way to attain it.

Two Winners in Every Discussion

A pleasant evening spring breeze wafted through the open patio doors as Miles Wignall, father of three teenagers, sat at his family room desk catching up on paperwork and bill paying.

"Miles, do you have a minute?" His wife, Lorene, had entered the room and put a hand on his shoulder. "Maureen says she wants to talk to us."

"Sure," Miles answered with only a touch of hesitancy but with a sudden jolt to his stomach muscles. Maureen was their eldest daughter, now eighteen, and Miles and his wife both knew what the subject would be. The daughter had been giving recent indications of wanting to get married.

They had discussed it before. Maureen knew her parents' views: she was too young, she hadn't gone with enough people to know the kind of man she really wanted, her boyfriend had no good career prospects—all the standard responses from parents of eighteen-year-olds.

"I'll get her," Lorene said.

"Oh, we can go to her room," Miles said, and they went down the hall and through the open doorway of Maureen's room.

Within a few minutes, it became clear that she was not announcing her marriage, at least not imminently. But she was anxious to determine how her parents would handle it if she should decide to go ahead with the marriage.

"I know you really don't want me to get married right now, and I'm not certain I want to either, but I also feel I'll have to make my own decision. I want to calmly talk it through with you."

"Sounds good," Lorene said.

"I think we can handle that," Miles added.

Lorene went on, "Before we really start, though, I'd like to say something. Your dad and I both feel we'd like you to wait. You know that. Yet we know we can't stop you if you decide to go ahead; you're old enough to make your own decisions. Of course, marriage is such a *big* decision.

"But what I want to say is: let's decide right now that this discussion and any future ones will end with you and us feeling like winners. Though you may go ahead and get married and we may still not be thrilled about it, or though you see it our way and decide to wait, let's plan right now that we won't end our talk with a fight, with rejection of each other, or with misunderstandings."

Maureen nodded as her mom went on. "You know we love you, and we know you love us. Let's keep in mind the whole time that even if we don't end up in agreement, we can still have had both sides express their honest views, we can still have weighed all the alternatives and consequences, and all of us can still feel like winners in that way."

How wonderful it would be if all family discussions could be handled with such mutual respect. How fortunate Maureen is to have parents who, in spite of their own strong feelings—even fears—about her early marriage, can let her know of their support for open, nonaccusatory, demand-free discussion. The fact that their daughter would come to them with a matter so ultimately personal, rather than merely announcing her decision, indicates that her family has practiced this approach for years. It pays big dividends.

Children need to know that most discussions can accommodate two winners and need have no losers. When a family adopts the attitude of no-loser discussions, the tone of family talks often changes from one of competition and combativeness to one of conciliation and reason.

When they're young, children won't always understand the idea that both sides can win, because if they don't get their way, they'll feel like they lost. Later, they will come to understand that they didn't really lose if their parents listened and understood and then had to make a hard and sometimes negative decision. In the long run, they'll see that a considered "no" is a sign of parental concern.

Manipulation: A Nasty Habit

"Honey, if you care about your parents—"

"Mom, don't use that line on me again!" Terry shouted.

"What line, honey?"

"You know what line. That 'if you care about your parents' bit. I have heard it so many times in my seventeen years I can't stand it. Plus 'in *our* family, we do this' or 'in *our* family, we don't do that,' like, once we're in this family, we can't exercise a choice anymore."

"Why, Terry, I—"

"Or 'don't let us down,' like you used on Jerry when he wasn't sure he wanted to go on a mission right away when he turned nineteen. Let *you* down? Was he going on a mission for *you*? That's the kind of thing I'm talking about, mom. You always try to work us around to doing things the way you want. There's only one right way for you, and you can't just state your view and let it be. You have to try to make us want to do it your way, like it was our idea. We all know what you do, mom. And when that doesn't work, you cry. I've seen you *make* yourself cry so people would say, 'OK, mom, I'll do it your way.'"

Wow. What is going on here? Terry certainly seems to have something to say and sounds like she has good evidence for what she's saying. True, she's upset and her phrasing isn't too careful and she's not being very respectful to her mother and there is always more than one side to a story. But what if she's right about her mother's manipulations? Is it acceptable for parents to manipulate their children—"work" them, as Terry calls it?

Some parents seem to feel manipulation is a gentler way of getting their way than being forceful and giving directions. However, it's still wrong. And it does have a cost. Not every child will see through it by ten, but most will by twenty. No one likes to be manipulated. When children realize they have been so treated, they feel cheated, robbed, demeaned. They feel that someone made them agree to things through less-than-honest means. They were trapped, pushed into a corner, and then made to give in—or feel guilty for not doing so.

Parents should say how they feel, and they have a right to be as persuasive as possible, but they mustn't "work" people to try to get them to agree to things for the wrong reasons.

Imperfect Families Can Produce Happy People

"I've called you together to make a special statement I hope will change our family forever." Dad addressed his wife and children in the living room one Sunday afternoon.

"I think, as a family, we've done pretty well. We seem to care for each other and help one another where needed. We enjoy doing things together, and we've had good times as a family. I think we've done fine up to now.

"But what I want to say today is that we need to do better. I've been reading and hearing in church about families who get along a lot better than we seem to. In spite of the many things we do together and the way we enjoy each other, we still

have our share of quarrels and "heavy"
discussions—your mom and I, we parents with
kids, and you kids with each other. I propose we
stop that entirely and learn to bite our tongues and
get along."

Marci moved further down the couch from
Christopher, who was jabbing her in the ribs just to
irritate her.

"I know it won't be easy, but I think if we all
try, we can learn to turn the other cheek. What do
you think? Can we, from this moment on, not have
another disagreement in our house?"

Dad has really hit upon an idea here! He wants to move
his family right from this telestial world to the celestial king-
dom in one step. We can sympathize with his desire. It sounds
so good. The only thing wrong with it is . . . everything.

It sounds like this family is already in pretty good shape.
They enjoy each other, they help each other, and apparently
they express their views—which, of course, sometimes results
in disagreements. If dad were to have said, "Let's work on a
better way to express our feelings so we can handle our differences more constructively," then we would say hurrah for
him. But what he has essentially proposed is that family members no longer express differences. He mistakenly calls it "turning the other cheek." Yet Jesus' admonition on peace certainly didn't turn him into someone without views or a
willingness to express them strongly.

No, dad has missed the point. Some psychologists have
gone so far as to say that "a fighting family is a happy family."
While this statement could be quite misleading—fighting does
not necessarily produce happiness—what is meant is that
people who rate themselves highest on happiness scales come
from families where people were allowed to express their opinions, even though such expression inevitably led to occasional
disagreements. Families in which differences were allowed to
be aired worked best. Those with emotional censorship—

which is really what dad has proposed—produced more angry, frustrated people.

A second conclusion of psychologists is that while striving for blissful family life is fine, to make it an absolute goal that *must* be attained each and every day is not so good. This approach generally results in unhappiness and guilt when everyday differences do occur. People then feel like failures. A better goal is to strive for family emotional "health" rather than "bliss." Health implies developing appropriate capacities for coping with differences and stresses rather than making pretensions that such things don't exist.

With these ideas in mind, dad's proposal is actually dangerous to the happiness of his family. Since people are allowed, expected, and certain to have different views, it's how those differences are handled that is important.

Being Interruptible

"Dad, can you help me with my math?" asks Geneal. "I don't know how to do it. Third-grade math is hard."

"Oh, OK, honey, but right now?" dad says as he pulls his daughter onto his lap. "It isn't even dinnertime yet, and I wanted to read this newspaper. How about after dinner?"

"OK. My teacher doesn't explain it well, and Paul—he sits beside me—bothers me all the time so I can't get my math done in school."

"Well, we'll look at it after dinner, then," dad says as he scoots Geneal out of his lap and opens the newspaper.

After dinner, the family watches an hour of TV. Then mom says, "It's eight o'clock, Geneal. Time for bed."

Geneal is in her pajamas before she remembers her math. "Oh, daddy," she says. "You didn't help me with my math."

"Oh, oh. We forgot, didn't we? OK, let's have a look at it."

As family communication goes, this encounter wasn't a grand success for dad. While he had a legitimate right to read the paper before dinner if that's his style, he may not have thought very far ahead about what the family might be doing after dinner. Still, the math got done, even if Geneal got to bed a little late.

In the future, dad may decide to postpone his newspaper reading until after the bedtime of his small children. He might also consider looking for opportunities to reward his diligent daughter who gets started on her work so early in the evening. What he may have inadvertently taught her is to postpone her homework until later in the evening, something he will inevitably find irritating as she gets older.

However, let's not accuse dad of any major infractions so far. Where he missed his opportunity is in the fact that he didn't really listen. By deciding to help his daughter later, he missed what might have been the key elements of her request. Geneal didn't merely need help with today's math. She also mentioned that she found her teacher's explanations inadequate and that she had a problem with her table partner. While these may or may not be major issues, an attentive parent would want to look into them, at least by asking Geneal for more details. But it seems doubtful that these points registered with dad.

It's perfectly acceptable for parents to postpone a child's request to better fit their schedule, where that can be reasonably done. But they must always be attentive to subtle references—which may turn out to be the main message and which may or may not be restated.

State Feelings and Listen to Those of Others

Mom was in her son's room talking to him about homework concerns. "So what I think you're saying, Michael, is that we are worrying too much about your homework and your recent grade report and not trusting you enough to decide for yourself how much time you need to spend on your own work. Is that what you think?"

"That, plus I feel your plan to restrict my activities won't work," Michael said.

"OK," mom said. "You feel like our plan to require structured homework hours isn't fair or necessary?"

"That's about it."

"Did I miss any points now?"

"No." Michael shook his head.

"Good. Now, let me state what I feel, and what I think your dad also feels. It's this. We know you think your semester grades will come out better than the term progress report. And you may be right. But we worry that you may actually not know *how* to do better. *Wanting* to improve doesn't always work. And if you have questions about why you got those C minuses, as you've said you have, then we wonder if you need either extra help or teacher conferences or something to get you on the right track again. That's our concern.

"Now, can you restate that to me, so we'll both be clear on what dad and I are worried about?"

Michael paraphrased his mom's concern to her satisfaction and mom went on. "I guess we're a little afraid for you, too, Michael. You're a junior. Your grades by the end of this year are the ones that will be sent with college applications. Yet you've slipped a lot over last year. I admit that we're scared that a lot of your options may be eliminated if you aren't careful."

"I know," Michael said. "But I don't think it will help to keep me in my room more, during these

new 'homework hours' you've proposed. What good
will that do?"

"Maybe no more than give you more time to
work and to let you know this is a serious matter.
It may not help, of course, since that largely
depends on you. But we think we have to try. What
would you propose?"

This conversation may lead to an understanding between
parent and child that will satisfy them both. If it doesn't, it's
not because they didn't try. Both parties are following a clear
pattern of listening, restating the other's views, and honestly
stating their own. These approaches tend to keep emotions
down and allow openness and progress toward a solution. In
a setting of emotional honesty and efforts to understand,
family members can learn to work things out together.

Such lessons carry over to the real world, too. People
raised in an honest, open environment are likely to grow up
knowing how to work well with other people. They've learned
that shouting and fuming aren't very effective in dealing with
others and that other people may have valid views. They've
seen that listening and reflecting, combined with straightforward statements of their own feelings, cause great leaps in
respect and understanding between people.

The most basic communication skill is listening, and it
takes practice, practice, practice. For those who haven't established a pattern of listening nonjudgmentally and reflecting
back to the speaker, it's very hard at first. How easy it looks
on paper, but how difficult it is to apply!

Who would have thought it could be so hard just to keep
our jaws clamped shut? However, it must be human nature
and is certainly social custom to immediately agree or dis-
agree with things people say to us. But neither of these
responses is nonevaluative. Using them will cause the other
person either to slant his remarks or to feel rejected—to react
rather than to merely proceed with expressing his feelings.

Parents who teach their children to listen, and who practice listening themselves, will develop in their family a basic yet profound skill in better communication.

Questions for Discussion

Do we encourage discussion in our home but also realize that "little ears" may misunderstand? How can we involve smaller children in the conversation at their level?

Do we encourage our children to talk about their feelings even when they need to bring up negative points about other people? How can we help our children understand that gossip isn't good but that from constructive discussions about people a great deal can be learned?

Is compromise a feature of our solutions to problems?

Are we certain we don't radiate hostility and rejection of our children when we disapprove of their actions?

Do we encourage the expression of feelings in our home, or is there an impression conveyed that certain kinds of things are not to be mentioned, thereby cutting ourselves and our children off from deeper understanding of one another?

How can we encourage the view that there can be two winners in virtually all discussions?

Are we able to avoid manipulation of other family members?

Do we accept the idea that the ideal family knows how to handle differences, not to cover them up and pretend they don't exist?

Are we interruptible? Do we recognize that key revelations may not be repeated at later sessions, so listening is important at the moment? Do our children know that if we can't help them or listen to the whole story at the moment, that we will set another time and keep the appointment?

What is our plan for practicing communication skills? How will we be sure our children learn these skills too?

6

Family Skills

Parents who think back to their youth can probably name several specific skills they learned from their own parents that helped them get along as a family. Some of these may have been directly taught, others perhaps assimilated without any direct coaching. Certainly keeping a family running smoothly takes many personal and group skills and attitudes. Some of them—such as that a home can be a pleasant place rather than a battleground or that chores can be shared, in this modern age, by both sexes—are attitudes or orientations more than skills. Attitudes are more difficult to identify, analyze, and teach than are skills—though they provide important components of happiness.

The few family skills listed here are not the most obvious ones. They are some of those often nebulous attitudes and skills that might be overlooked for the more practical, yet no more valuable, skills of daily living like politeness, kindness, and hard work. Budgeting, goal-setting, and learning to take responsibility are surely as vital to our children's long-term success as learning to cook and clean. Many of the skills and viewpoints parents teach will carry over to the time when the children leave to start their own families. Therefore, attention to the little things will start a positive trend affecting many generations.

Money-Handling and Financial Planning

When Taylor came to his dad to talk about buying a better bicycle, it came as no surprise. All spring, Taylor's Varsity Scout troop had discussed taking a cross-state bike trip later in the summer. And, clearly, Taylor's old bike would never make it. Or, more accurately, *Taylor* would never make it, since his bike was a small-wheeled BMX-type with no gears.

"I'll need a mountain bike for this trip, dad," he said. "That's what they call these new heavy-wheeled fifteen-gear bikes, like in this picture." He handed his dad a catalog and pointed to the bike he had in mind. "They're bigger and bulkier than ten-speeds, but they're lightweight and they pedal real easy," he added for the sake of his dad, who might not be up on the latest in bicycles.

"And," Taylor added, "they're very expensive." Dad looked at his son and waited. "The one I want is about $280. Some of them are $600 and over."

"Two hundred and eighty dollars for a bike?" dad exclaimed. "Yes, with tax and the accessories I'll need for the trip. But I can sell my old bike, and so I figure I should need only about $230."

"Only, huh?" dad queried. "I see you have it all figured out."

"Yeah, I do." Taylor looked pleased.

"How much do you have in 'spend'?" dad asked. All of his kids had been taught to pay their tithing first, save half of the rest, and put the other half in what they called their 'spend' fund. And he knew Taylor was good at saving up his 'spend' for big items.

"Well, only about $20 or $30 right now 'cause I got my skis," Taylor answered. "But I have a plan."

"Oh." Dad enjoyed his son's confidence. "Let's hear it."

"Well, it's that you buy the bike and I pay you back each month out of my paper money. I—"

"Uh, uh," dad cut him off. "That's no plan at all."

"Or," Taylor was undeterred, "You could charge it and then I could pay the payments to—"

"That's even worse," dad said.

Taylor was silent.

"I think you'll just have to wait and save up the money like we've always taught," dad said.

"Dad, I can't save enough in four months. And I need the bike for the trip or I don't need it at all."

"I think that's more bike than you can afford, Taylor. You could get by with a used ten-speed or something."

"No, dad. That won't do it."

"Well, son, if you can get the money by then, fine. But I won't charge it."

Dad knew something about Taylor's determination—sometimes called stubbornness—in situations like this, and over the next few days, Taylor and his dad talked several times. Dad suggested getting a job in the early summer, before the trip, to supplement the paper-route money, though he knew that would be difficult for a fourteen-year-old. At first opposed to any kind of charge plan, dad came to see that there might be a way to help Taylor get his bike and also help him learn fiscal responsibility. First, he discussed the idea with his wife.

"I suppose most other parents would just let their kids take the money out of savings. But we've always called our kids' savings 'mission money,' and I hate to let Taylor start at fourteen to spend it on other things. He bought his skis and boots without using it.

"So here's my idea. Maybe we could let him borrow from his own savings—let him take the money out of savings and pay it back monthly to the credit union. That plan might even have a byproduct—helping Taylor get out of his system the idea that credit is so easy. When he sees most of his paper money committed for the next several months, he may not like borrowing money quite so much."

Mom agreed the idea had merit. And Taylor was thrilled. He used his cash, sold his old bike to his younger brother, and borrowed $200 from himself, committing to repay his own account at the credit union at $25 a month for the next eight months.

Here is a positive example of how children can learn, under the direction of parents, to handle money in mature ways. Children can learn from their earliest years that income isn't to be frittered away on the first toy or piece of candy that meets the eye, but is to be divided into church offerings, savings, and spending money. By the time they become old enough to miss the amount put into savings, they have accumulated quite a lot, but they have learned it is not to be spent now. Young people could make major contributions toward missions and college if their parents established in them the saving habit early.

Those savings can also be a boon along the way as a source of funds for occasional large purchases. A realistic borrowing and repayment plan like the one Taylor used helps children enjoy immediate benefits from their savings as well as helping them understand the pinch of repayment. The latter may be one of the most vital lessons parents can teach in today's "easy credit" society.

Chores and Sex Roles

Mom was frustrated. Her twin boys had always done their share of household chores along with the girls. Then, in their early teens, the boys had suddenly decided they were no longer interested in "sissy work."

"You can reassign us all the outdoor stuff," Jeff said. "And taking care of the cars," Jay added. "And maybe, if we had to, we could vacuum for indoor chores."

"Yeah, I guess we could vacuum, if none of our friends knew about it," Jeff said. "But forget dishes and laundry and scrubbing sinks and stuff. Things like that—with your hands in water—that's girls' work. We don't do girls' work anymore, mom."

As upbeat as teens try to be and think they are, no segment of society is more outdated in their views of masculinity and femininity. No group on earth is more interested in establishing an exaggerated and stereotyped macho image than teenage boys, and many teenage girls seem incredibly tied to traditional feminine views, as well. Establishing their own gender identities seems most important at this age.

The speech Jeff and Jay gave their mother might have been standard for any period of Western civilization prior to the last few decades. Today it merely sounds quaint. Apparently unknown to the twins, the day is largely past when women's work and men's work were so easily differentiated.

Most dads today believe that they have a larger role in child-rearing and household chores than their fathers believed themselves to have. Therefore, parents who don't see to it that their boys know how to cook and clean are handicapping them for the future. While the twins' mom may have to make adjustments to help her boys past this image crisis, she should not give up entirely and let them escape regular household chores. They will someday very likely need to accept similar tasks as their duty as family members and fathers.

Home Can Be a Pleasant Place

"I think you'll all like to hear a note from grandpa that came in the mail today," mom announced as the family enjoyed the sunset from their patio.

"Read it to us, mommy," said Merrill, age five.

"OK. Well, first he tells about their trip home and how they found everything fine there. And there's a note from grandma, too, that we can read in a minute, but grandpa wrote the part I want you to be sure and hear. Here it is."

I want to thank all of you for the wonderful week mom and I spent with you. We learned to get to know our grandchildren better, whom we never get to see often enough.

I want to say something to all of you about your family. I've noticed this before when we've visited but never more than this time. It's simply that you have such a pleasant atmosphere in your home. I'm not sure how you do it. Maybe it "just happens" because of the good people you are. Oh, I know you kids have your little spats at times, and you all certainly have strong wills and your own opinions on things—which is good, incidentally. Still, you all seem to go out of your way to be helpful, kind, and pleasant with each other.

Perhaps some of what we observed might have been because your grandparents were visiting for the week. Maybe you were putting on your best manners for us. But I think it's more than that. It's obvious that you really care about each other, and that you take time for each other. These things aren't easy with the busy schedules you all have. Such concern for others is certainly not the case in every household these days.

Keep it up, and thank you so much for letting us visit you.

Love, Grandpa.

Of course, families put on their best behavior for infrequent visitors. And maybe grandparents see little angels where parents see mere mortals. But in some families, pleasantness is the regular order of things. In spite of busy—even hectic—schedules, parents and children get together often for talking, helping, nurturing, and just plain sitting around watching sunsets.

Grandpa knows full well that pleasant home atmospheres don't just happen. Deliberate effort is necessary to establish routines for having meals together, praying together, reading together, and spending time getting to know one another. Planning is required to organize family chores so people know their tasks and realize their contributions are important without requiring harping parents to push them unwillingly into work. And leadership and commitment are essential to create a parent team that is clearly in charge but that still allows an open and relaxed atmosphere where children feel they belong.

These "little things" take effort, yet they pay big dividends in raising children who become happy, productive, tension-free adults. On the other hand, the typical "American-style" dawn-to-dusk dash may turn the home into a command headquarters rather than a pleasant refuge. When this happens, children and parents come to use the home merely as a refueling stop, losing sight of its real purpose.

Excitement, Variety, and Boredom

"Do you think Nadine needs this, too?" asked Arthur.

"Well, so many of her friends are in the group that she really feels left out," answered his wife, Renee. "Besides, she's bored with her flute lessons."

"Bored? Already? After we just rented a flute and spent money on a month's lessons?"

"I don't like it either, but you know how they are at this age, Arthur. They don't stick with things very well."

"The child is thirteen years old. It seems time she settled down to *something*. How many activities has she been in and out of in the last four or five years? First, there was the junior drill team—the 'strut team,' I call it—then the two kinds of dancing lessons, besides clogging. Then she started piano, the group singing lessons, the violin, fifth-grade orchestra, sixth-grade band—some of which lasted no more than two weeks. There were Girl Scouts, 4-H, ski class, even soccer and softball."

"She's flighty, that's for sure. She really is interested in a lot of things," Renee said.

"Yes, for about twenty minutes," Arthur said with disgust. "Now we're into junior cheerleading, aerobics, and flute, which she now wants to drop, to be replaced by the baton squad you say all her friends are in. What has she *ever* stuck with?"

"Not much."

"She can't play a note on any instrument she ever started, she shows no interest in dance—she's simply never stayed with anything. As soon as something gets hard or demands concentration, work, or practice, she's 'bored.' I don't like it. I think she's now learned to be the same way in school. That's why she's not doing well this year. She simply won't persist in anything that takes longer than a baton lesson."

The pressure is heavy on modern parents to provide "broadening," "enriching," and "exciting" opportunities for their children. And, in themselves, many of these activities probably are worthwhile. Even though youth don't always continue with them, there still may be value in sampling various activities. A person certainly doesn't have to become a professional to have benefited from sports, nor become a concert performer to gain from music education. But when sampling becomes more important than completing or continuing *anything*, there is a problem.

Parents may find themselves providing a life of distractions rather than substance. Then their children may never learn that most meaningful achievements require a certain amount of monotony, repetition, and hard work. Bertrand Russell described it as "fruitful monotony" and maintained that it is essential to happiness. Only if people at times turn off the outside amusements can they discover the quiet— even idle or boring—moments in which to come up with constructive plans, goals, and desires.

We live in a world where TV has encouraged a short attention span. Producers know that a wandering mind will soon change the channel, so commercial shows are generally produced with flash and variety as main components. (Notice how most teenagers react to educational shows on public television. "How boring!" they say.) Any schoolteacher can verify how hard it is to compete with such variety and visual diversity. Unfortunately, to some children, books are a drag for the same reason—books just sit still in the hand instead of jumping around and singing. "How boring!" they say.

If parents feel compelled to provide their children with constant variety, excitement, and stimulation, they may be doing them a great disservice. Children need to learn to stick with things, even boring and difficult things, and to look within themselves for meaning and substance. Parents must avoid turning their children into social "flutterers" who hop impatiently from activity to activity without staying long enough to develop persistence, depth, or lasting interest in any of them.

How Long Will Children be Dependent?

The panel of three college students had made
opening statements to Mr. Adams's high-school
personal-finance class. The subject of their visit was
how they had learned to handle money. Now it was
time for questions from the class.

Shortly there came a question from the back of
the room about parental support. "How much are
your parents helping you with college?"

Stephen answered first. "I live at home, and my
folks pay my tuition and books. I have a part-time
job so I pay for my own clothes and dates and
things."

Michelle was next. "I'm probably in about the
same situation. I work summers and save nearly
enough for my school expenses. My folks pay my
housing, most of it, since I'm from out of state and
can't live at home like Stephen does. Since I'm planning to go on for a medical degree, I will need a lot
of help for quite a few more years."

There was a pause before the third panelist
answered. He seemed almost embarrassed with
what he had to say. "Well," Alan said at last, "I
don't get any direct support for college."

"You must have a scholarship," a student said.

"A partial one," Alan answered. "It covers half
of my tuition."

After a pause, Mr. Adams said, "You must
work, then. Or else you're independently wealthy."

"I wish!" Alan smiled. "Yes, I work. I've been
paying most of my own way for years, even in high
school, as far as clothes and things. By the time
we're eighteen at my house, that's it."

"I'm glad I don't have *your* mom and dad!"
This response from a class member brought a laugh
from the rest of the students.

"That's what I used to think, too," Alan said. "Then I came to be proud of what I could manage on my own. Now I wouldn't want it any other way."

"What do you mean 'when we're eighteen, that's it'?" someone asked.

"Well, my parents are really not mean people. But they told each of us kids about the time we turned thirteen that they would expect us to be adults at eighteen. Not that they would kick us out then; they just expected us in our teenage years to learn to take care of ourselves, not only in money, but in everything. They started giving us more and more responsibility and expecting us to make decisions.

"I noticed back then that a lot of my friends didn't have it this way. And sometimes I felt a little cheated. But not for long. Even then I was amazed that many of my friends' parents bought them cars and gave them all kinds of money and got them out of scrapes I never got in—partly, I guess, because I knew it would be up to me!"

Alan paused again, feeling he was monopolizing the time.

"Tell us more," Mr. Adams said.

"Well, I think the thing my folks tried to instill in us is the idea that we were capable and, at least by eighteen, should be able to make pretty good decisions on our own. After all, by that age, you can vote, get married, join the armed services—all without parental permission. So, is eighteen adult or not? Well, my folks taught us it was. And they expected us to act like it."

Alan shook his head and grinned. "I've really been going on here. Let me get back to the financial question. I don't think it's necessarily *bad* for a parent to help someone through college." He glanced at his two partners at the table. "I realize there are lots of different circumstances. My dad says, 'It isn't wrong for parents to help their grown kids. What's wrong is for the kids to expect it and for the parents to feel they have no choice about it.'

"So they told me to find my own way to get through school. There's a junior college in my hometown, and I could live at home when I went there, of course. Dad said, 'If you need to work summers and evenings, that won't hurt you. If you have to lay out a semester to get money ahead, even that won't kill you.' And that's probably what I'll have to do if I go on to graduate school. I'll need a break from school about then anyway. They told me to try for scholarships, and student loans if I needed them. So far, I haven't had to get a loan.

"So, I don't know how many of you agree, but I think it's a great way to go. I learned a lot from it, and I'll definitely raise my kids this way."

This approach is not a cop-out for parental responsibility. It's a calculated, gradual way for parents to teach children responsibility while they're still at home where parents can rescue them if necessary.

This is an eminently reasonable alternative to the more common modern approach of keeping kids in the financial nest through the age of twenty-five or thirty or more. Alan may not have convinced most of his high-school audience, but he could surely convert a few parents.

The concept of gradually increasing independence doesn't apply only to finances but to all decisions. An early start on this idea will be met with a positive reception by teens because they sense they are being given more freedom even though it comes with greater accountability. They like the feeling of being in charge of themselves.

Parents also love the approach for many reasons. As a teaching tool, it can't be beat. And it avoids the resentment many parents feel when their "required" support of their children seems to go on too long.

"It's just so hard for kids to get established these days," some say. But it's no harder than ever. It's just that some people define "getting established" rather more generously than in earlier days. Some parents not only put their kids through school but buy them cars, send them to Europe, and make down payments on houses along the way. And not a few parents feel they don't have any choice about it.

Of course, "adult at eighteen" does not appeal to those parents who define their own security and worth in terms of controlling their children—whether at five, fifteen, twenty-five, or thirty-five. Some parents fill too many of their own needs through their children.

For the sake of their children, parents need to teach them to work for what they get and allow them practice in decision-making. In these "little things" children learn to handle the bigger things of the future. Young people thus prepared find leaving the nest less of a shock than do those who have never before tried their wings. (See Jim Sanderson, *How to Raise Your Kids to Stand on Their Own Two Feet*, New York, Congdon & Weed, 1978.)

Goal-Setting: The Way to Get Somewhere

"So, Matthew, how are we doing this week?" Mom and her son were meeting for their weekly goal-review session. "Did you bring your notebook?"

"Yep, it's right here," Matthew said as he produced a small spiral-bound book. "First, I'm up to where I'm supposed to be on my music."

"OK, I've noticed you're keeping up really well. It's helped a lot to write out your goals, hasn't it?"

Matthew nodded.

Mom asked, "Music is your number 1 category, right?"

"Yep, and number 2 is Scouts. For that, I wrote down that I would finish my second-class award by the end of the month. I finished the first-aid merit badge at the powwow, so I have only two more, and I'm halfway through one of them."

"Sounds good. What will you have to do to finish on schedule? Or, I should ask first, do you still plan to finish by the end of the month?"

"Oh, yeah, I'll make it. I'll start the citizenship badge this week, and in Scouts Tuesday, we should finish the cooking badge."

"Great."

"Then number 3 is my money goal. I'm a little behind on my goal to save $20 for Christmas presents. I forgot to count exactly what I have, but it's only about $8. So I don't know if I'll make that."

"Let's look at how much longer you have and what ideas we can find to help out with it—that is, if you still want to shoot for that. You may not need the whole $20, you know."

At eleven years old, Matthew already understands that goals are important in helping people stretch more than they otherwise would. With a good set of goals, children soon see growth and progress in themselves, and they learn valuable, lifelong lessons about the power of goals.

Brief weekly meetings may be necessary to keep children reminded of what they have decided to do. Parents can also help children avoid setting goals that are too difficult or too easy.

Weekly meetings should be short, unpressured, and open for discussion and modification of plans. Matthew writes his goals in a simple notebook—which will be very useful for his self-esteem as he looks back over goals he's attained. The goals are set by the children, the parents just act as helpers to keep them on track.

Caution: While a little goal-setting, appropriate to age levels, is good, it doesn't necessarily follow that more is better. Too much pressure can be applied to children to excel. Parents should give their children guidance in realistic goal-setting but still let them be kids too.

Questions for Discussion

How are we doing at helping our children learn to budget for the things they want?

What is our family's attitude about household chores and sex roles?

How would we rate our home for pleasantness? Are there things we could do to improve the atmosphere?

Are we being driven excessively to provide variety and amusement for our children? Are they inadvertently learning to become samplers rather than completers? Are they being conditioned to demand constant entertainment and so miss out on some of the advantages of a certain amount of quiet time?

How do we feel about letting our children become adults at age eighteen? Are they appropriately independent for their age? Are they growing in their ability to take care of themselves, or are they too dependent on us?

Do we help our children to set realistic goals and to progress toward completing them?

7

Life Views

We've all known people who radiate constant anxiety and worry. They seem miserable, and they make those around them miserable. Of course, these people feel that their many concerns are logical and reasonable, and somehow they're convinced that worrying helps the situation, which is about as evident as that knocking on wood keeps away trouble. To these people, life is a sneaky and fearful opponent that must be watched constantly to prevent a stealthy attack.

Another class of people spend all of their energy working for the future, failing to realize that life is passing them by right now. Some of them never lift their eyes to enjoy the sunrise, the sunset, or anything in between because they are so diligently planning and working for tomorrow. Tomorrow's sun comes and goes and they miss it too—toiling for the next day.

These two traits—excessive worry and missing out on the present—are examples of life views that make a great deal of difference in the way people travel through this world and how they feel about the journey. Often people who fall into such traps are totally unaware of the price tag their attitudes carry. And one of the main uncounted costs of negativism and anxiety is that parents with these tendencies unknowingly lead their children into the same dark paths.

Think of what a different life they would lead if the chronic worriers were able to see how futile most of their concerns were and decided to accept life as an enjoyable challenge instead of an onerous burden. How much different would be the lives of those who procrastinate living if they decided to, at least now and then, stop to pick a buttercup, order an extravagant flaming dessert, or read a story to a child.

In this chapter, we'll examine a few ways of looking at life that may make a great difference in how much children enjoy their time on earth.

Life Can Be an Enjoyable Challenge

"Dad," Travis said, "Karl's dad got laid off today at the plant. Karl said quite a few others did. What does that mean about you?"

"Well, I made it through this cutback—and the last one. But the future of the plant doesn't really look too great." Dad leaned back in his chair and put down his fork. "Maybe it's time I said something to all of you about that."

The family listened expectantly.

"You already know that things are scaling back at the plant. We've seen this coming for two or three years now. I'm in a different job than Karl's dad, so I'm safe for now. But I decided quite a while ago, in talking with your mother," nodding at his wife across the table, "that we would try to be in charge of our own situation as much as possible, and not be totally dependent on somebody else's decisions.

"I know I could be out of a job in the next year or so. But your mom and I have always taken the view that we can sit around moping or we can look at this possibility as a challenge to overcome. That's how we've tried to look at everything in our lives.

tude, you can still enjoy the challenges—though not always at the moment."

"Like when you broke your foot and couldn't drive for two months, dad?" Gene, the ten-year-old with a wry sense of humor, said. "I'll bet you didn't enjoy that challenge until it was over."

"No, I sure didn't. But I've worked at the plant for fourteen years. In that time, we've had three or four major threats of layoffs and closures. I've seen guys I work with make themselves absolutely sick about it. And what good does it do them?

"So I decided I would prepare myself through night classes for other options, and I'm still doing that. I believe in thinking ahead; I don't believe in feeling sorry for myself.

"It wouldn't be easy if I were laid off, but we would make it. I guess that's what I mean by taking life as a challenge. We just do our best to handle and even enjoy what comes. Things somehow work out."

Certainly there are times when life is a pain and a half and when all the positive thinking in the world won't make the hurt go away. In fact, sometimes such thinking can be so unrealistically blind as to actually make the pain worse, because it keeps us from admitting and facing the problems we might otherwise do something about.

So a head-in-the-sand approach is not the answer. However, parents who can help their children see life as a challenge—tough but positive and enjoyable, like a game where we play a few rounds each day—will help those children better get through life without being beaten down. How much happier are such people than those who always feel oppressed by circumstances they think they can't change.

We Can Always Do Better

Tim and Lorna were looking over their family budget sheets again.

"You know, Tim," Lorna said, "when we started a budget a few years ago and you said you wanted to handle it, I thought you would keep more careful track of where the money was going. Now, wait, I know that sounds accusatory—"

"It sure does." Tim winced.

"Well, without attacking you, I do want to figure out why we keep coming up short. That's when *I* feel bad is when we're so short that regular food and household expenses make the budget run over. I think it's that so many things don't get recorded that it's never clear where we stand. I thought that was the idea of the budget."

"I don't know. I guess I just forget to write some things down. Of course, not recording them doesn't *cost* us any extra—they're still just expenses we needed to cover anyway."

"I know, Tim, but unless they're written down, how can we track them and know if they're really legitimate? And especially, how can we know how much money we've already spent?"

"Maybe you'd better do the budget, Lorna." Tim sounded a bit agitated.

"I'm no good at it, Tim. I hate it," Lorna protested. "But I still think a budget is necessary, and since you're the one who's had business classes, we decided right at the start you should do it. I'm not trying to take it away from you; I'm not saying I could do any better. I just feel we—you—need to write *everything* down."

"I'm just busy and I forget. Really, I do the best I can, Lorna." Tim said exasperatedly.

Later in the evening Tim found himself talking with his sixteen-year-old daughter about her household chores.

"You don't seem to keep up anymore, Amy. It isn't fair to the rest of us."

"I know, dad, but I'm busy at school and things."

"Yes, and we've made adjustments for that. I don't see any reason you can't do these simple little jobs you have so others don't have to wade through the mess you were supposed to clean up."

Tim was surprised to hear Amy repeat a line that sounded rather familiar: "Dad, I do the best I can. That's all I can do."

We nearly always deceive ourselves when we claim to "do the best we can." It sounds so good, so unassailable, the perfect excuse. And sometimes it even happens to be true. But seldom. Most of the time, what it means is: "I'm doing things the way I've always done them and I don't want to change."

Very rarely do people ever do their very best on a given task, at least not over an extended period. We all get into our ruts, and even though we may work hard and keep busy, that's not the same as doing our best. The fact is that we could almost always produce better results if we found better methods.

If Tim had a better system, he could keep a better budget. If Amy organized her time better, she could keep up on her chores. Therefore, these two are not being quite accurate or honest to say they're doing the best they can. They may be doing their best under the particular limitations they've put on themselves. But with a new way of looking at things, with better systems or planning, they would do better work. Therefore, their "perfect" excuse is none at all.

Tim needs to ask his wife to help him come up with a better way of handling the budget. Amy needs to ask her dad for suggestions for organizing her time to include her chores. Then they might be a little closer to accuracy when they say "I'm doing the best I can."

Accepting Rejection

Martha was heartbroken. The sight of her daughter hunched on her bed sobbing had nearly moved Martha to tears, too.

"Oh, honey, I wonder if there could have been a mistake in the counting or something." Martha felt that she had to grasp at straws to help LeeAnn feel better.

"Mistake?" The word did seem to get LeeAnn's attention. "How could there be a mistake? Unless . . . unless someone cheated at the ballot box." LeeAnn reached for another tissue and sat up on the bed.

"There were three voting places. And, come to think of it, I noticed that two of those boxes were staffed by Laurie Hiatt's supporters." LeeAnn's eyes narrowed. "I'll bet they could have stuffed the boxes or something. I always was more popular than Laurie Hiatt. It doesn't make sense that she would beat me as sophomore class secretary."

LeeAnn was beginning to see the possibilities of this idea and felt better already. "I wouldn't put it past them. And you remember I told you some of my posters were taken down last week. See? They knew I'd win so they *had* to cheat. Oh, what does it matter now?" She sank her face back into her pillow and wailed. "It's too late now. I've already been humiliated."

Martha's sorrow had now metamorphosed to anger. "It's never too late. I'm going to that school."

"What?"

"Come on, wipe your face. We're going to talk with that principal about his sloppy election procedures that allow cheaters to win!"

School had been out for an hour, but Martha and her daughter found most of the staff still at work. They were directed to Mr. Cutler, the assistant principal, who had supervised the elections. His explanations that each of the ballot boxes had been staffed by students but overseen by one of the full-time adult employees of the school didn't seem to impress Martha. She insisted on counting the ballots herself.

Mr. Cutler reluctantly allowed her to do this. When she was finished, her count of the sophomore ballots matched exactly the official count: Laurie 96, LeeAnn 82. Martha then insisted on speaking with an employee who had watched over one of the boxes and had her explain the whole procedure about the locked box that only the assistant principal could unlock.

"Then what about the removal of my daughter's posters?" Martha challenged. "Doesn't that constitute cheating? How can you let people get away with things like that?"

"Well," Mr. Cutler answered patiently, "there are two things to know about that. First, it's true that a few posters were removed last week, belonging to several different candidates. We don't know who did it, so we could only notify the candidates the next day and allow them to replace the posters."

"But I didn't have time to make more," LeeAnn protested.

"I understand," he said. "It wasn't your fault that vandals took down the posters, but there seemed nothing we could do other than allow new ones to be put up. It didn't seem directed at any specific candidates. Incidentally, I noticed in the outcome that at least two candidates whose posters were removed—including Laurie Hiatt—still won."

Martha didn't like that. "Something should have been done."

The man ignored her remark. "I mentioned," he said, "that there were two poster matters. The unauthorized removal is number one. Maybe LeeAnn didn't tell you about the other."

"What do you mean?" Martha asked.

The vice-principal looked at LeeAnn and waited. She wouldn't look at him, so he said, "Mrs. Smith, the candidates were all given a printed copy of the campaign rules early on. One of the regulations had to do with the size of posters and where they were allowed to be displayed. Well, two of LeeAnn's posters had to be removed by our own office staff because of violations of those regulations. She was also notified of that."

Martha looked at her daughter, who merely shrugged. "I didn't think it would matter where I put the posters."

"Well, I suppose a girl has to do something to get ahead of the cheaters," Martha said as she rose. "Come on, LeeAnn." At the door, she turned to Mr. Cutler and said, "I think the whole thing needs further investigation. My girl worked very hard for the election. She's clearly the most prepared candidate, not to mention the more popular of the two girls. I don't know but what the school board ought to look into this matter."

Although Martha may be teaching her daughter a great deal about pushiness and immature histrionics, she is teaching her very little about how to accept life's inevitable rejection and disappointments. In fact, Martha's approach hinders LeeAnn's acceptance of her defeat. By Martha's insistence on carrying the matter beyond where reason or evidence merits, she is teaching the worst possible response to rejection—avoidance.

Psychologists join the voice of common sense in telling us that letting the truth sink in is the first step in getting over a grievance. How many people have held on to a wound for years, whether in romance, employment, or family relations, until it finally consumed them. Rejection of reality can only make one bitter, not whole.

We're not talking, of course, about legitimate concerns or misunderstandings about which something can be done. We're speaking of those things that are over, done, and finished, over which we have no further control. Our blame of others, self-recriminations, wailing, and groaning all have no effect other than to keep us too-long focused on the problem and, frequently, on our self-pitying sense of unjust suffering. It's then that "little things" truly become huge.

Peer rejection will never be fun for youth or adults, so LeeAnn is allowed to feel sorry and to wish things had gone otherwise. But she must put a limit on her sorrow, accept her loss, and move on. This is particularly true of the type of failure that is the result of rejection by others. There was only a limited amount that LeeAnn could do to win the election; after that, it was up to the voters at the ballot box.

If Martha had found evidence of cheating, that would be worth pursuing. But there was none—other than that attempted by her own daughter in violating the poster rules, but Martha justified that in her own mind. What she can best do for her daughter at this point is to help her accept the fact that she lost the election—that neither the school board, the governor, nor the Royal Mounted Police are able to change that fact—and that life goes on. There is, of course, personal growth to be gained from any experience if the attitude is right. But the first step is acceptance.

Everything Has a Price

Greg had owned his car for six months when he said to his dad one evening, "Dad, I have a transmission problem."

"You *do*?" dad asked with a grin.

"You know I mean my car," Greg grinned back. "The mechanic says it's not unusual in a car of this age. I heard it whining so I took it in."

"What's it going to cost you?"

"It's hard to tell until Sam tears it down, but he says not less than $100 and not more than $400."

"Wow. Welcome to the world of car ownership, my boy."

"Dad, you don't seem to be taking this very seriously." Greg's grin had faded.

"I guess I know it's not my problem, Greg," dad replied. "I do sympathize, though. That's a lot of money."

"Well, I was wondering . . . " Greg started.

"How is it I can feel a 'dad, can you help me?' coming on?"

"Dad, I don't have $400. I've got about $100 without dipping into savings. And—like you'll be quick to remind me—we agreed I wouldn't use savings after I got the car."

"I'm glad your memory is working so well, Greg. I was hoping not to have to come up with one of those nasty 'I-told-you-sos' about how we talked about the cost of cars not being only in the initial cost."

"I know, dad, but I didn't plan on this."

"Of course not. However, when you could only afford an eight-year-old car, you knew you needed to plan on *something*. That's why an 'I-told-you-so' *was* forthcoming a few weeks ago when you bought the new cassette deck and four-way speakers. In a car of this age, if it hadn't been the transmission, it would have been something else.

"Well, enough lecturing and reminding. Maybe you'd better let Sam look into it and then decide what to do. Maybe you'll be lucky and come out toward the low end. If not, you may just have to wait."

"And not get it fixed?"

"Not until you can afford it."

"Dad, surely you could loan me—"

"Could? Of course I *could*. But *would* I? That's the question. And I'll bet you can guess the answer. And do I feel guilty? Same answer."

"Dad!"

"Listen!" Dad cocked his head. "I think I'm starting to hear that whine you described."

What a tough one dad is today. Greg is experiencing one of those painful moments we all have when we find out what it's like to run right into life headfirst. All of this was predictable, of course, when his folks tried to talk him out of buying a car in the first place. But the enthusiasm of youth won out. Now comes the time to face the fact that all things have their costs.

Not always are those inevitable costs in money. Sometimes they involve time, effort, sorrow, lost opportunities, or other uncountables. But often, the costs are in cold, hard cash—never colder or harder than when we need it and don't have it.

If Greg's dad is able, he will hold out against his son's importunings so Greg will learn a lesson that can usually only be learned the hard way. When parents feel themselves weakening, they need to remember that the hard lessons children so much want to avoid in life's small matters have a way of making things a lot easier for them in the inevitable bigger troubles of their future.

Worry, Worry

Stan rolled over, turned off the alarm, and pulled back the drapes for a look outside.

"I hope it doesn't rain—or snow—before I get home from work, Grace. I've got to rake the leaves and mow the lawn one more time this fall."

"It doesn't sound good," his wife said. "Last night's report said the storm could come in by this afternoon."

"Rats! I hope not. With the leaves down, it will be a mess. I'll have to keep the radio on at work to see what the report is."

At breakfast, Stan said, "Gee, I hope the mortgage rates drop today so we can refinance the house. I lay awake half the night hoping for that drop that's been predicted."

"Me too," Grace said.

After Stan left for work and the kids for school, Grace planned her day. "I hope the oven will work right tonight," she thought. "I want to do a roast, and it's been acting so erratic."

During the morning, Grace wondered how her seventh-grader was doing on his math test. "He's such a worrier that he got himself all worked up about that test," she thought.

By two o'clock, heavy snow was falling, the first of the season. "I'd better pick up the girls at school. They'll get cold otherwise."

The girls had other ideas. "Mom," Cindy said, "all the kids are walking home in it. It isn't cold. You made us carry our coats all fall. Now we can finally wear them!"

"Yeah, mom," added Luann. "It's the first snow, and I want to make tracks in it."

"No, girls. You might catch colds. You come with me in this nice warm car."

Stan's first words when he came in the house were, "This snow bothers me. I listened all day, and they said this would happen. Now the leaves will smother the lawn. I wonder when it will warm up again and melt. I'll worry until it does. Let's see if we can catch the weather report tonight."

At supper, Grace said to the family, "I sure hope your sister doesn't get any of those parasites missionaries sometimes get in that part of the world. She was worried sick about that when she got her call. And I've worried about it all day."

"Mom," Cindy said, "you haven't stopped worrying about that since the day she left."

That night, Stan, Jr., had plans to go to a party. After Grace had him list for her all the people who would be there, she asked him who was driving.

"I'm walking. The party's only at Jon's house. It's six houses up the street, you know."

"Be careful, son. I'll be waiting up, you know."

"Mom," he said, "We're only watching a video. I'll be home by 11:30."

"I know, son, but you know I just can't sleep while any of my kids are out."

Grace must surely be labeled a concerned, considerate mother. And Stan is nothing if not an anxious man watching over his money and his yard. While these traits have their admirable aspects, these people have a major problem, do they not? They spend their time in that most unprofitable of all pursuits—worry.

Worry has been called "low-grade fear." And, of course, certain things in the world are clearly to be feared. But so many of the petty things people torture themselves over are not worth the trouble. Unless Stan is planning to come home early to beat the storm, why worry about it? Either it will snow or it won't. Wishing for a decrease in the mortgage rates isn't bad either, but is it worth lying awake all night worrying about something he has no control over?

What about mom's fears about the oven, the math test, and the possibility of her daughters' catching colds? How helpful was it to worry about parasites all day? And *must* a mother wait up while her teenage son is six houses down the street for three hours?

Are concerns and anxiety part of the requirements for parenthood? Well, a certain amount of worry does seem to come bundled up with the parenting package. Since we're so fully invested in our children, since we so much want them to be safe, happy, and successful, we have a right to be anxious about their whereabouts, their health, their choices, and their accomplishments. Still, many parents go too far with their inherent right of worrying about their offspring.

For one thing, worriers often have little discrimination and seem to worry about everything with equal fervor. Is it any surprise that an offspring of Stan and Grace "got himself all worked up" about his test? Or that another "worried herself sick" about an aspect of her mission? Children tune in very quickly to fear, and fearful parents radiate a constant if low-level apprehensiveness, which creates a new generation of fear-laden and timorous people.

Either-Or Thinking

"I tell you, Connie, if that guy gets elected, this country will collapse."

Connie looked at her husband, who was obviously very agitated. "Clint, are you sure he could do all that much damage? After all, the president doesn't have all the power, you know."

"I tell you, with his ideas and his warped view of things, he will bring in his type of clowns to help him, and that will be it. There will be no stopping it. The man's a crook and probably a junkie, too. Either he loses or the country's had it."

"Well . . . " Connie started to speak, but her son Steven entered the room. "Mom, dad, I have a problem."

"Yes, son, what is it?" mom asked.

"It's Clark."

"Oh?"

"He's driving me crazy. How can a ten-year-old have so much junk? I didn't keep my room like that when I was his age. If he doesn't keep his side of the room cleaner, he's got to go back to the baby's room. I never would have let him move in with me if I had known how it would be."

Dad said, "Have you talked with him about it?"

"Only a hundred times. It does no good. Either he cleans up or out he goes. You told me when he moved in it was just a trial." Steven left the room.

A few minutes later, Clark came in. "Mom, Steven is acting like a maniac. He says I have to get out of *his* room. He says he's going to throw my stuff out in the hall."

"Oh, dear," mom said. "Tell him to come here right now or he's had it."

As he started down the hall, Clark called back, "Either he keeps his hands off my stuff or I'll dump over his dresser."

In this household options seem to be in short supply. People here apparently don't know there are often many positions between fast forward and full reverse. This kind of "either-or" thinking gets a lot of families in trouble. Ultimatums are set and discussion is ruled out: "It's either that dog or me; one of us has to go—today!" "Either you do your share around here, young man, or you start paying rent." "If you can't keep your stereo turned down, I'll take it away from you."

Analysis and intelligent conversations are eliminated by statements like these. In their place, defiance often sets in:

"Go ahead, who cares?" Then difficulties get out of control with results no one really wanted. Either-or thinking in interpersonal relations sets up the necessity that someone lose.

Parents who talk in either-or terms shouldn't be surprised to hear their children doing the same. It will take a concerted family effort to discover that there are nearly always reasonable midpoints where resolution is less radical and more satisfying than either the "either" or the "or."

Life Is Now

"Grandma, do you have any advice for our birthday boy here?" Cal asked his mother as the cake was being cut. Ruth thought she'd long since become used to being called grandma by her own son, but now and then it still startled her that she was one of the progenitors of a forty-three-year-old father of five, all of whom sat around her table now.

"What can an old woman tell a seventeen-year-old?" she grinned.

Todd, whose birthday the gathering celebrated, said, "Quite a bit, I'll bet, grandma."

"That was the wrong answer, Todd," Grandma teased. "You were supposed to say, 'Oh, grandma, you're not old.' "

Todd laughed. "Well, I'd probably take advice from you better than from my folks."

"That wouldn't be saying much," his mom said.

"Well, since you're begging," Ruth Cartwright said, "there has been something on my mind lately that people ought to keep in mind, at seventeen or any age, I think." She paused as if to be sure her audience was interested.

"Yes?" Todd asked.

"You go on cutting that cake, Todd. Don't let my speech slow you down or your little brothers and sisters will be sorry they came. Oh, mercy, I forgot to get out the ice cream. Cal, it's right there in the freezer."

While Todd cut his birthday cake and placed the pieces on grandma's blue china plates for his dad to add the ice cream to, Ruth started: "I think it's pretty simple advice, but, like all advice, easier to hear than to do. It's just this: remember that life is now."

Todd glanced at her, unsure of her meaning. She went on. "When your grandpa and I were young, we were both raised on dry farms where money was about as scarce as rain in July. Our folks taught us to work hard and to get ahead and maybe someday things would be better. I think neither of us really knew anything except work.

"And so, when we got married, we found ourselves in a similar situation. Times were tough, and there we were trying to do the only thing we knew how to do—farm—the only way we knew how to do it—hard work.

"Cal, don't be too dainty with the size of that serving. You know I love chocolate pecan."

"From what I've seen, mom, there aren't too many kinds of ice cream you don't love," Cal said.

"Never had it when I was young," Ruth said. "I'm making up for lost time."

Ruth went back to her story. "Anyway, don't take what I'm saying too far and decide to lay back like the grasshopper and take it easy. There's a time for hard work, all right. But sometimes I think the ant is a little silly too, the other way. I look back and I think we were too tied to the place—there was always something to be done, or sixteen things to be done—and we didn't know how to enjoy life as we went along.

"I'll eat while I talk. And you all go on and eat too. We don't want melted ice cream.

"Your grandpa was the hardest worker I ever saw. He put his heart and soul into it. And I was about the same, I guess. At times, though, I would hear about a dance in town or about people we knew, who had no more than we did, saving up to take a little trip or something, and I wished we could do it too. But we were always too tired or too broke or too behind on this or that. At least that's what we thought then.

"And that's how we raised these babies, your dad Cal and the others. They learned to work, they did. And that was great. But I remember your dad, here, asking his dad to take him fishing. It was a drive across the valley to the river, and we let Cal go with his friends a few times. Arlie was always saying he would take him, too. Then every spring we'd be so busy, and then, before we knew it, a few weeks into summer, the river would get low and the fishing was no good. I don't think he ever took you, did he, son?"

"No, mom, he never did," Cal said quietly.

"Well, I guess that's about it, Todd, and the rest of you. Work hard and set goals and make plans for the future. But you remember that an old woman told you, 'life is now.' Cal, is there any more ice cream?"

Ruth has it right. Life is now. It's like a long train going past. People can get on it anytime they want, but one thing is sure—it will only come by once. If they spend all their time toiling beside the tracks, too busy to do more than plan for the day they will climb aboard and start their trip, they may entirely miss the train—and the point—of life. In the midst of teaching our kids to work hard, to save money, to

135

get good grades, to do all those good things that will help ensure their future, we must also teach them that life is now.

This view has perils, of course. It's not always easy to know when to lay down the hoe or the pencil or the vacuum and head for the fishing hole, the museum, or the skating rink. It calls for balance, and some will inevitably put their heavy thumb on the scales and tip them too far toward the pleasures of the moment. A few will abuse the concept and claim they "need a break" when they haven't broken into a sweat in a month.

But there's no more danger in that—maybe less—than in becoming a workaholic or one who is always "just getting this one job done" before having any fun. "This one job" soon turns into another and another and another, people never quite manage to break away, and, meanwhile, the train is chugging on by and picking up speed.

In one of life's most important "little things," parents must help their children find the balance between working for the future and not missing life at the present.

Questions for Discussion

How effectively have we taught our children that life can be an exciting challenge in spite of difficulties, that it can be like a game we're determined to have fun at? How much do we believe this ourselves?

Do we use the phrase "I'm doing the best I can" as an excuse not to listen to constructive criticism or to new ideas? Can we help our children not to hide behind this delusion?

Can we better teach our children to handle the inevitable disappointments and rejections in life? How can we help them face their losses and then get on with other things?

How good are our children at looking at the costs of their decisions? How can we help them do better?

Are we compulsive worriers? Do we see signs that our children are worriers? How can we better help them to avoid fretting about the things they can't do anything about?

How much do we think in narrow, preconceived "either-or" terms? How can we help our children see alternatives to the extremes at both ends of the scale?

If life is now, how are we enjoying it as a family? Is life getting away from us while we keep ourselves too busy to enjoy it? How many opportunities are we missing as our children grow up and away from us? Do we see trends that indicate our children know how to balance working for the future against enjoying the present?

Are we convinced that it's the "little things" in our home that make the difference? How will we help each other to be aware of the effect even our smallest actions may be having on our children?

Index